Grieve

Stories and Poems
about Grief and Loss

Volume 6

HUNTER WRITERS CENTRE

Grieve Volume 6
Hunter Writers Centre
Newcastle NSW 2300

Email: publishing@hunterwriterscentre.org
Website: www.grieveproject.org

Grieve: Stories and Poems about Grief and Loss

22 21 20 19 18   1 2 3 4 5
ISBN-978-0-9954409-7-5(paperback)

Cover design by HWC Publishing
Typesetting by HWC Publishing
2018 Published by Hunter Writers Centre Inc.

© Each short story/poem is copyright of the respective author
© This collection copyright of Hunter Writers Centre

All rights reserved.
No part of this publication may be reproduced, stored in a retrieval system, or transmitted in any form by any means electronic, mechanical, photocopying, recording or otherwise without the prior consent of the publishers.

Table of Contents

Blood and bone — 1
Justine Hyde

Not Horses, or Mothers — 2
Lisa Jacobson

A Day in October — 3
Kim Waters

Time — 4
Alyssa Sterry

One Word — 6
Rob Selzer

Would haves — 7
Naomi Deneve

The Skeleton — 8
Nicole Melanson

The Line Our Thread — 9
Cynthia Troup

Heartbeat — 10
Emily Usher

This big bright land — 12
Simone King

The day after coming home from hospital — 13
Claire Watson

Hot and cold — 14
Belinda Oliver

What About Me? — 15
Samantha Noble

Tough Love — 16
Barbara Hunt

Let Me Introduce You . . . — 18
Vanessa Farrer

Hashtag — 19
Karenlee Thompson

The little ones — 20
Christine Kearney

I Have the Weight of a Life that is Substantive and Real on my Shoulders — 22
Sook Samsara

Knitting, Endings and Grieving — 23
Anne Boyd

A hard won Spring — 24
Tahra Baulch

Sometimes, Love Isn't Enough — 26
Louisa Simmonds

Fells Philip Radmall	27
Black News Anthony Levin	28
a black point Niko Campbell-Ellis	29
Bendalong Michele Seminara	30
First season Jane Gibian	31
A Japanese Airman Forewarns His Wife B.R. Dionysius	32
chemo days Trisha Pender	35
Cairo Natalie Holder	36
No-one is ever really gone Tim Hardy	38
Blue Karen Wickman-Woldhuis	39
Broken Decima Wraxall	40
Those Days Sarah Bourne	41
Debt for Life Barbara Rosie	42
A tea-rose for Frieda, *Deutsche Shäferhund* Louise Wakeling	44
I wish I knew Helen Angela Taylor	45
Custard Lindsay Watson	46
Ashes Gillian Telford	48
burial Connor Weightman	49
Motherless Daughter M. Fletcher	50
Ultrasound Lisa Jacobson	51
Circumference of desire Jenny Pollak	52
Residue: a small amount of something that remains after the main part has gone Judy Mullen	54

Camp David Thérèse Murphy	56
Circumspection Paul Hetherington	58
Custodian Norm Neill	59
Dear Diary Richard West	60
4pm Sara Crane	62
A Letter Anahata Giri	64
Choosing Gail Hennessy	66
Comfort Steve Evans	68
Ether Jo Withers	69
Lost Jacqueline Damen	70
Eulogy Grace Dwyer	71
In black and white Ian Wicks	72
Blue Deb Godley	73
Everything I need to know (letter from a widow) Susan Bradley Smith	74
Grieving is Overrated Mark Bromhead	76
Even Richard James Allen	78
Family portrait Grace Dwyer	79
Fairy Dust Louise Baxter	80
Farewell to Billy Duluth Lesley Carnus	82
Not Long, My Darling Audrey Molloy	83
A Love Letter To My Little Sister in Prison / A List Of Things I Didn't Say Because I Was Afraid Trixi Rosa	84
Detritus Joan Katherine Webster	87

Guilty gratitude Christine Burrows	88
Super Hero Fiona Everette	90
How it is Alison Flett	92
Everywhere Jo Gardiner	93
Cold Karen Lieversz	94
Looking for Clark Gable Alexandra Geneve	96
In the Quiet Moments Emma Pasinati	98
Indwelling Ron Pretty	99
My Dear Son M. Wong	100
Let it not be this Jennifer Chen	101
Resting Bitch-Face Thérèse Murphy	102
On the hottest midwinter day on record Peter Lach-Newinsky	104
My Elisa Alexandra Geneve	105
Maracas Trixi Pavey	106
Scenes from a Hospital Kate Ryan	108
memoria in aeterna Sandie Walker	110
Intermission Jenny Pollak	111
One Lump or Two Billie Ruth	112
Since you Beth Spencer	113
Yiayia Sibella	114
Time for Grief Seetha Nambiar Dodd	116
Not Crying, Dancing Linda Stevenson	117
Where has my family gone? Michael Cole	118

On My Mum's Passing Belinda Paxton	119
Renovations Sylvia Muller	120
words out my mouth Kathryn Lyster	121
Skin and Bone Melissa Manning	122
Some time later PS Cottier	123
Sirens Meg McNaught	124
Two Trees Tanya Richmond	126
There are days Penny Lane	127
Vincero I will overcome. Merran Hughes	128
The Stone Jar Chris Lynch	130
Still Lauren Forner	132
Stuff going on while I'm paying rent Glenn Aljatreux	134
Small Things Cameron Langfield	136
Tears Marianne Hamilton	137
Try Judy Mullen	138
Fathom Nicole Sellers	139
Why I can't talk Eleni Hale	140
Three Unbearable Things Helen Richardson	142
the lactic acid in the calves of your despair Ali Whitelock	144
The Hobs of Drought Jan Iwaszkiewicz	145
Grief Is Kim Anderson	146

*The sun was about to rise—
not quite dawn,
but somehow no longer night.*

- From *The Skeleton* by Nicole Melanson

Introduction

Another volume in the Grieve series; another stirring collection of poems and stories that capture, with brilliant clarity, the confusing, blurred, often overwhelming, experience of grief. This anthology has many works about death and dying but also stories and poems about other losses: loss of career, loss of a pet or loss of a long held dream or hope.

The Grieve Project continues to attract new voices and established writers. It is thrilling to see first time writers published alongside writers who have honed their craft for decades. Some pieces will leave you gasping and in awe of both the subject and the words used to convey that subject. Many will move you to tears and it is hoped all the works may help you reflect on the losses you have experienced and those to come.

Karen Crofts
Director
Hunter Writers Centre
Australia

www.grieveproject.org

Awards

The National Association of Loss and Grief (NALAG) Award
Blood and bone by Justine Hyde

The Australian Centre for Grief and Bereavement Award
Not Horses, or Mothers by Lisa Jacobson

The Australian Funeral Directors Association Award
Time by Alyssa Sterry

The National Association of Loss and Grief (NALAG) 2nd Award
A Day in October by Kim Waters

The Australian Centre for Grief and Bereavement 2nd Award
One Word by Rob Selzer

The Australian Funeral Directors Association 2nd Award
Would haves by Naomi Deneve

Lifeline Award
The Skeleton by Nicole Melanson

Palliative Care Australia Award
The Line Our Thread by Cynthia Troup

White Lady Funerals Award
Heartbeat by Emily Usher

Good Grief Award—for a work about grief or loss other than death
This big bright land by Simone King

All About Grief Award—for a work about grief or loss after the death of a child
The day after coming home from hospital by Claire Watson

David Lloyd Funerals Award (Newcastle and Hunter Valley)
Hot and Cold by Belinda Oliver

Suicide Prevention Australia Award
What About Me? by Samantha Noble

Simplicity Funerals Award
Tough Love by Barbara Hunt

White Lady Funerals, Mayfield Award
Let Me Introduce You by Vanessa Farrer

The Compassionate Friends Award
The little ones by Christine Kearney

The Calvary Mater Hospital Pastoral Care Award
I Have the Weight of a Life that is Substantive and Real on my Shoulders by Sook Samsara

The Blue Knot Foundation Award
Hashtag by Karenlee Thompson

Mindframe Award
Knitting, Endings and Grieving by Anne Boyd

Hunter New England Health, Mental Health Services Award
A Hard Won Spring by Tahra Baulch

Hunter Writers Centre Award
Sometimes, Love Isn't Enough by Louisa Simmonds

Hunter Writers Centre Members' Award
There are days by Penny Lane

Highly Commended Awards
Black News by Anthony Levin
Fells by Philip Radmall

Special Mention
Lost by Jacqueline Damen

Blood and bone

Justine Hyde

She wants to thump her body into blooming bruises and rip her insides out and spill her loathsome intestines and organs all over the betraying earth, throw herself down on the black dirt and pound her fists until they bleed and fall apart and dig her hands into the soil so her fingernails split down to the quick, to scream eternally from the pit of her soul and tear the stinking grass out of the earth by the roots and slam her useless head until her skull smashes open and her brain splits into a million rotten atoms and becomes sludge and stops torturing her, to dig her own grave with her bare hands and bury herself deep under the layers of seasons and suffering, suffocate herself with thick mouthfuls of humus, clog her lungs with sand and silt and fill up her eyes with quartz and turn to the sky to let the crows peck them out, to welcome the crawling worms and the fat slugs and curling slaters and creeping ants into her body to consume her piece by piece, to let the creatures pick her flesh from her bones and strip her skeleton clean, so she is just a pile of collagen and calcium and phosphate decaying into granite and crack her bones open and spill out the marrow, let it pour out with her blood and seep into the basalt and limestone, be carried away by floods and winds, washed into a river and spat out into the sea, swept far south to the pole and become frozen into a glacier and melted by the warming oceans, evaporate into the sky and condense and rain down as a torrent onto this treacherous place.

Instead, she stands silently and watches as they lower the tiny coffin.

Not Horses, or Mothers
Lisa Jacobson

Mother, whose life is almost spent,
we no sooner arrive than you are readying us to leave.
Our names fall through you like water through a sieve.
Migration is inevitable.
On the river whose far bank is unknowable
there's a boat with your name on it.
The water birds stand on one leg and shiver their wings.
The blank-eyed fish kiss the tide's underbelly.
The horses lower their muzzles to drink.
Nothing lasts, not horses or mothers.
Meanwhile, the wind runs across the fields,
the wind runs across the fields.

A Day in October
Kim Waters

It was an odd sort of day to take her leave,
The wind faltering in the tulle curtains
She'd sewn when they first moved into the place,
A day that wasn't certain of its own purpose,

As though all that it had come to believe
Of itself was suddenly in doubt
And in the face of dying had lost its nerve,
Preferring to keep a polite distance.

She lay, as she'd never done before, stately
Under an embroidered bedspread, her hands
Fanned beside her, her skin turned
To wax in the light of the late afternoon.

Of course, we gathered, as family do,
Around her bed, silent and poised,
Waiting for the last bullet of breath,
For the pendulum in her chest to stall

In its motion. We expected to hear bells
When it was over, but none came.
It seemed as though she'd just excused herself
For a moment and walked out of the room

Leaving us there with our stony feet,
Unable to meet each others' gazes
Because if we did we would have to admit—
She was never coming back.

Time
Alyssa Sterry

Recently, I've found myself wishing for more time. But also for time to speed up, so the pain doesn't have to be felt for so long. I want more time to enjoy with the people who I know have to leave. Time to enjoy their company, learn their stories and sit in their presence just a little longer. I want it to work for me. More of the good stuff that makes life so amazing, while speeding up time when life is painful and almost unbearable.

Time when the reality that they're really gone, sets in.
When the final goodbye has been said.
When the ache in my heart grows and grows until it feels like it may burst.
When it's harder to get out of bed in the morning or return home because they used to be there.
When the fear of facing the grief appears bigger than the need to heal.

I just wanted more time. More time to enjoy her and know her. Or maybe just less time feeling the pain, now that she's gone.

I've done 'grief' many times in my life. And I've often done it differently. The first few times I didn't know any better. Later, it was because I had learnt something that allowed me to grieve differently. Sometimes, I ignored my grief because the task of letting go seemed overwhelming. I even saw my pain as a way to stay close to someone I had lost. My pain couldn't be bad as it reminded me of them. That belief chipped away at my heart, at my hope that I could heal, that life could get better.

And now, after all I've learnt, I still wish for an easier way, a less painful way. While I miss all I have lost in this life, it is time that I miss the most. I've never had any control over it. I've never had enough of it, or sometimes I've had too much. Too much time alone, in silence, to feel the depths of my grief and my heartache.

I met time the other day.

She listened while I told her what I believe I need from her for a better life. I told her how she has always given me too much and sometimes too little of herself. I yelled, angry that she couldn't see what I needed.

But she said, 'There is always enough. Enough of me to appreciate what you have and enough to heal when there is loss. It's your choice what you do with the amount I give you. You can embrace the time when you're grieving and use it to heal or you can find a way to distract yourself from the pain. This may help for a while but it will leave you with even less than you have been given. Less time to feel, to process and to be set free. It's always your choice how you use it. So choose wisely. Your heart depends on it.'

One Word
Rob Selzer

Some words commit murder. Hanging in the air, then a hard punch to the guts, their pain is physical.

Sorry.

There it is. Heard it a thousand times. But right now it is coming at me from a stern looking doctor with greying temples, my dad's age. He holds my gaze with heavy eyes, trained not to look away, and he speaks slowly, in a voice made from gravel. I picture the word sine-waving the two metres between us; from his lips, sailing over the cream linoleum, past the fading Monet print, into me. He shakes his head as if wanting to rid the aftertaste, the finality.

You don't hear as much as feel them, those murderous words, because oddly they are silent. Maybe it is because our ears, suspicious of their intent, block them out. But they creep in under the skin.

My stomach heaves and I have to hold back from retching. The lino sways in front of me. I am sea sick. But I am uncertain if it is from his *sorry* or from the smell of the Eucalyptus deodorizer losing its battle against the rising tide of vomit wafting in from the corridor.

He repeats himself and I hear it loud and clear now. But my insides have already registered its impact. I can't help it and my mouth fills with sharp mucus. I spit into a tissue and apologize. He nods. He has seen this a thousand times.

Peta is in the room too, sleeping. I fully expect her to spring open her eyes just like she did this morning, kiss me and disappear into the shower. *Lulla-bye*, she'd sing flying out the door to work, the scent from her apple-blossom shampoo lingering. *Lulla-bye*, I'd call back. It was our private joke: *Good-bye's* are too final, but a *Lulla-bye* blankets you in a blissful reminder of someone you love.

Except now there is a tube poking out of her mouth. Connected to a hose snaking over to an appliance that looks like a washing machine, it is pushing air into her lungs with a metronomic rhythm; she is a rag doll held onto this side of life by a contraption that looks more at home in our laundry. She'd love the irony – *What do I have to do to get you to do the washing, Ben?*

Glioblastoma Multifome, he says, and then explains that the tumour has been hiding, growing undetected in her brain. Today it declared itself by puncturing an artery. She would have laughed at that. *A tumour in my brain? Hah! I feel fine.* But then maybe that's a blessing: she never knew.

I use the walls to help me across to the bed. I stroke her beautiful, washed hair. I lean over and take in its fragrance. I kiss her. Putting my lips to her ear, I take a deep breath and whisper, *Lulla-bye.*

Would haves

Naomi Deneve

Loss changes everything. Especially words. Suddenly you no longer have the privilege to speak these words about him.

Will becomes would have. He would have turned 27. He would have liked this podcast. I wonder what he would have said when Trump was elected. He would have been so pleased I'm donating blood.

The first time you catch your self saying would have instead of will it chokes out of your throat, each sound scraping as it makes it way out. It's a change the others don't even notice. But for you it changes everything. It has taken away possibilities. It has marked the finality of it all. Four siblings has now three. And as you say the would haves your brain creeps into the could haves.

What could have helped? What could you have done? Could this really be as endless as it feels?

The would haves mark the start of the grey time, where every sound is muffled, every colour dampened and every feeling muted. You move slowly with laboured steps. And then suddenly within this grey, a word reaches out and assaults you, throwing you to the ground and knocking the air from you. Words that you never noticed before now leave you winded.

But so unremarkably slowly the would haves change. Something around them softens. There is a gentleness that lingers around what were once such jagged words. To have known and loved him so well that you can say with certainty that he would have done. To remember him so clearly that you know what he would have liked. To be able to explore how he would have thought about something just from the many hours spent with him. A slow warmth builds. You learn that he will be with you. Standing by your thoughts, decisions and dreams. And you will be ok. Knowing that he would have stayed if he could.

The Skeleton
Nicole Melanson

Be at peace now, they said,
when they finally found my child.

The sun was about to rise—
not quite dawn,
but somehow no longer night.

I used to watch the light
change in her eyes and know
she was going to smile
right before she smiled.

The wind was waking too,
making the trees sound like laughter.

They didn't know any better.
It was barely spring.
The leaves were immature.

That's the way it goes in Nature—
one day you're naked,

the next you're dressed all in green,
weaving a nest
and dreaming of eggs.

They asked if I wanted to see her bones.

When I choked, *Yes*,
they showed me an empty birdcage.

The bird was nowhere to be seen.

The Line Our Thread
Cynthia Troup

Last night I spoke about you to another friend,
remembering our last phonecall, when you were too weak
to hold the handset to your ear on the pillow
and the blue nurse, as you called her,
the home carer, pressed the speaker button so my voice
could be heard stretched and floating
on the bedsheet beside you.

My friend and I talked about how, once in a while, we can know
absolutely when it's the last time, we can come to know
when, for instance,
the silk strands that tether the dying are lifting,
and our loom with the dear one will soon be still.

The blue nurse, as you called her, omitted
or forgot to switch off the speaker button, replace
the handset in its black cradle. Perhaps
because I didn't say goodbye, as such;
I had said *thank you*, quietly,
imagining January sunlight striped by shutters in your room,
the sweep of the ceiling fan,
Ollie the Labrador by the bedframe,
scents of the flowers that filled the house
distilled with magnolia blossoming outside. I knew
there was a bunch of peonies in a tall glass, the verandah was dusty
from the Queensland storms, that as your breathing
had become inaudible the soughing of palmtrees and the high-set house
seemed calmer, deeper, in crescendo.

It was up to me to ring off from the phonecall, lose the line
our thread, rest my handset in its silver cradle
and keep talking, holding
the peonies, embracing Ollie, blessing
blue nurses and the wordless wisdom of the morphine drip.

Heartbeat
Emily Usher

'At this stage in the pregnancy we would expect to see a heartbeat.'

Her voice is kind, but her words do not make sense. They bounce from my skull like hailstones from a windscreen. She places the probe back on the table and peels off her gloves, and I see the way her stomach swells underneath the fabric of her pale green dress. She catches my eye. Blushes.

'I'll leave you to get dressed,' she says.

I don't know how I find my way back to the waiting room. Every corridor looks the same. But somehow I am there. A television blares from its mount in the corner. There is something wrong with the dubbing; the sound and the picture are all out of whack. A newsreader announces a fatal stabbing in Sydney's west and a blonde presenter throws her head back in a silent laugh, her shiny pink lips stretched taut across bright white teeth.

An eternity passes before the doctor calls my name again. She is young. Younger than me. I doubt her instantly. They've got it wrong, this wouldn't be the first time. She wants to explain my options to me she says. She would recommend surgery, but of course, it's my choice. I place a protective hand on my stomach, you cannot hear this. You are there, you are mine. I feel you.

I need to leave this place with its words and terms that I do not want to understand. Expected . . . medical . . . surgical management. They are for someone else, they're not for you, it's all wrong.

That night I lie in bed with you. I will you to live. I will you with all my heart and soul, I believe you can do it. We are one and the same and I believe in you.

The next morning the bleeding begins.

Physically, you do not bring me any pain. You slip away without complaint. You surprise me in that way and I am grateful to you for that. But with you, you take a piece of me.

A week later. A different sonographer this time. Perhaps they don't let the green dress lady see people like me. She tells me it is good news. My uterus is empty. There is no need for any further intervention. I marvel at her choice of words . . .

'Under the circumstances, this is the best outcome we could have hoped for,' she says. I wonder if I am supposed to feel grateful.

She keeps talking. My chances next time are good. No increased chance of miscarriage, most women will go on to have a successful pregnancy and on and on and on. But I do not care about next time. It is you I have lost. I want you.

On the way out I pass the hospital chapel. I am not religious, but something draws me inside. It is quiet and calm and peaceful.

I sit down. My head falls to my knees.

You are gone.

I let the tears come.

This big bright land
Simone King

Remember the trip over?
Us, pressed against windows, little mouths open
ready to gulp in the vast blue Pacific
filling more space than we knew the world contained
shimmering as confidently as the Milky Way
Us, flying hand-in-clammy-hand
over the chapped moonscape of this great land

Brother, I wait for you
in a grey room whose walls reach for me
sticky stains that smell like dog piss
they lead me along the long, lightless hall
a confused chorus of male voices
yelling pleas, greetings, insults
bounces off cold concrete

When I look at you
wide hollow eyes, meatless cheekbones
wispy limbs eaten by sores
I see faceless ghosts
the ones we thought couldn't cross the Pacific
followed us here
headless uncles lying in the street
screams shattering the surface of the night

Then here, ghettos of grief in cluttered housing blocks
no words, no care, no help, no jobs
just quick, cheap fixes
you inhabited a smoky haze
with off-white air so thick, so foggy
hard human shapes couldn't form

They will send you back to Timor
they will say you failed to comply, you didn't fit
the shadow you cast is too long
for the bright light of this place
And I'm afraid you will wander alone
in a place children tried to forget, but could not
calling no names, holding no hands

The day after coming home from hospital
Claire Watson

For Hannah

While the sun kept shining as if nothing had happened,
I was standing under the clothesline in the backyard, seething.
The cars were rushing past beyond the fence, everyone on their way somewhere, but
I wanted the whole world to stop, for one moment pay attention,
because our two year old daughter had just died in my arms. It felt reasonable
to blame God, who had allowed the goldfish to survive in our absence. I was so angry,
I longed to smash the fish tank on the concrete. I wanted
to express the unfairness of life, that's why.
To express the unfairness of life, that's why
I longed to smash the fish tank on the concrete. I wanted
to blame God, who had allowed the goldfish to survive in our absence. I was so angry,
because our two year old daughter had just died in my arms. It felt reasonable
I wanted the world to stop, and for one moment pay attention.
The cars were rushing past beyond the fence, everyone on their way somewhere, but
I was standing under the clothesline in the backyard, seething
while the sun kept shining as if nothing had happened.

Hot and cold

Belinda Oliver

'Don't tell your mother,' he says, taking a drag of his smoke. The tobacco crackles, glowing red as he breathes it deep down into his lungs. I'm not sure if he's asking me or telling me, so I say nothing. I just nod. Smoke wafts past me and I watch as the tiny cloud evaporates into thin air, as if it never existed. He's been chain smoking since this morning, when she said she wanted a divorce. I see the trails his tears have left, winding their way down the sides of his face and running under his chin. His cheeks are reddened from the crying and I imagine his eyes are stinging, aching with rawness.

'Where'd you throw it?' I ask him. 'Round there somewhere,' he says, pointing a metre or so away from the bank. It wouldn't matter if he knew the exact spot anyway, I think. The ring is gone forever, settling into its new home deep amongst the rich, brown clay of the dam floor. I remember when we were younger, my sisters and I smeared that very same clay all over our bodies and faces, much to our mother's dismay. It never fully washed out of our clothes, which were left with pale brown splotches afterwards.

I throw a pebble into the water and watch as ripples spread across the surface, creating miniature waves. I remembered how the water temperature here could change so quickly. One minute you could dip your fingertips into its murkiness and feel as if your submerged fingers were being sliced off with the sharpest of blades, the cleanest of cuts. Yet only moments later you could dive into the depths of it and find surprisingly warm patches to loll about in. Just like my mother changing her mind, I think, as indecisive as that. Hot and cold. Yesterday she wanted to work on their marriage. Today, she wants a divorce.

'What's she doing'?' he asks. I don't want to tell him the truth - that she's packing her bags. So I lie to him.

'Watching tv,' I reply. 'She told me to come find you. That you'd probably want to talk'. At least that part is true.

He gives a small laugh, or maybe it is a grunt. I can't be sure. 'And here we are,' he says, lifting his hand as if presenting the dam to me the way you proudly present a gift to someone.

'So . . . what now?' I ask. Our border collie Jesse nudges my knee and Dad grabs a tuft of his fur and begins pulling at a matt in it.

'Stuffed if I know,' he says, grinding out his cigarette on the dusty earth. He drags the butt across a rock, leaving a black smear of ash. He buries his face in Jesse's fur and sobs; a deep guttural sound I have never heard before, one that I never knew he was capable of making.

What About Me?

Samantha Noble

I have a story, and I know that everybody does. I hear them too, the daily tragedies on the news. The destruction of lives and the families left behind. And although loss is awful for the victim's family and friends, it can also leave a mark on others.

My story is a little different. What happened to me is the story that nobody ever tells. The story that nobody ever thinks to tell or even asks about. I didn't know the man. I was just a stranger. But he planned it. He planned it to be me. I know what he was thinking. A stranger wouldn't care, right? A stranger wouldn't suffer? He was wrong.

It's been three years now and still I have to fight each day. I didn't need to know him to feel the loss. I didn't need to know him to dream of him. I didn't need to know him to live with his pain.

Imagine it, wife, kids, business, day to day life. You speak to him a few days prior, organising the job. He tells you on the phone to let yourself in, he'll be working in the garage. In my profession it's not uncommon to be in and out on paint day. So you let yourself in and head to the garage. Suddenly, because of this man, this stranger who planned it, your life is in turmoil.

It was too late to help, I knew that. I knew it the second I saw him, but they didn't, those on the phone. I couldn't help.

They came.

They took him.

I told my story.

I went home.

That was the end of it. Nobody called to check up on me, nobody offered me help. Was I supposed to move on, supposed to just forget about it?

What about me?

The psychologist says it's trauma but I already know that. What I'm feeling now is guilt. Guilt for my family. For my wife and kids that I have been absent from. For how close I have come to ending this journey for myself, without them ever knowing it. I know that if I choose that path, I too will be passing on the pain but hell, it's tough to live.

He awakened a dark and ever present place inside of me. He pulled it to the surface, not knowing or simply not caring what would come of my life.

So here I am, finally telling the story of a stranger, the stranger you never think about.

He planned it. What about me?

Tough Love
Barbara Hunt

He gazes at me. Stares at what I am wearing. The sight of my joggers excites him and he staggers out of bed. His eyes, clouded and weary, plead, 'Take me with you. I can still do this.'

I grab his leash and he trundles beside me, stopping to sniff the grass. He pees and I look in horror at the stream of crimson, undiluted blood streaming onto the ground as he empties his bladder.

I have to make a decision. I know about the tumour, but I thought we still had a few months left together.

Rex loves to ride in the car, but I feel like a traitor, knowing that I am betraying his trust. The only consoling factor is that this journey is more difficult for me than it is for him.

We enter the waiting room. I sit - he stands beside me. The pit of my stomach is hollow and I feel nauseous but I force a smile at the teenage girl cradling her puppy.

She nods at Rex. 'He's very old.'

And sick, I feel like adding, but say, 'He's thirteen.'

We enter the consulting room. He explores. His nose twitches with excitement as he slowly moves around every inch of the room.

The vet and her assistant enter the room and his tail wags in recognition. He resumes his sniffing as we discuss the non-existent options for his future. Satisfied that we are all making the right decision, the two women leave the room.

It gives us a little more time together. I crouch beside him, hugging him for reassurance that I really am making the right decision.

'You were our protector and guardian. Do you remember how devastated Mum was when Dad died? She would have been lost without you.'

He leans against me and stares, cocking his head as he studies my quivering lips and misty eyes.

Tears stream down my cheeks as I throw my arms around his neck. He gives me a quizzical look and licks the saltiness away.

'Everything is easier for me if you are here,' he seems to say.

Even your death? I wonder.

The ladies re-appear and it is only then that he looks fearful as they both converge upon him, one holding a hypodermic syringe filled with blue liquid.

'Reassure him, pat him,' the vet says.

I hold his face in my hands and stroke his nose. 'Remember that I love you,' I say to him.

A look of bewilderment fills his eyes as the needle enters his front leg and the vet depresses the plunger.

I see his life ebb before me and he slumps to the floor, before all of the deadly liquid has even left the syringe.

'We'll be back soon,' whispers the vet. The door hushes shut behind them.

I close his staring, lifeless eyes and stroke his muzzle one last time.

Let Me Introduce You . . .
Vanessa Farrer

Did we pay for the consultation? I can't exactly remember, but we must have. It is after all the contract you have with service providers, even if the service is not at all what you hoped for. I do remember that the receptionist, who was also the wife of the specialist, thanked us. As she did so, she wore an expression of genuine consolation, which only made her look self-conscious, knowing frankly as she did, that any consolation was impossible. We in turn thanked her, playing our part in the polite exchange of social manners, and made good our escape into the outside world.

But outside is no longer the same. The sunny afternoon brings no relief. There is no air to breathe. No warmth to feel. Everything in my chest is falling into the deep pit of my stomach. My stomach then bungy jumps down into some deeper ravine. My stare lingers too long at things I cannot see. My gaze shifts but nothing changes.

A crack materialises that in time will become a great gulf. A gulf that will eventually tear us apart. We cling to each other and weep, each in our own universe of pain, our minds simultaneously traversing the millions of eons of everything that will be gone. We hold on tighter.

Later. Finally, a moment alone. The primal physicality of grief descends. An avalanche of pain falls through my body, as if seeping down through the ages into my blood. My crumpled face held by sodden palms, ribcage heaving up and down. I am doubled over with disbelief *and* comprehension in the same instant. My head tosses wildly from left to right frantically trying to loosen the grip of this new reality.

I am a cat, flying through emptiness, scrambling to untangle all the bits of myself and land feet first on the ground. Only there is no ground. I can't land. The ground has vanished.

I am free falling, flailing in infinity. Time, space, solidity, substance, all fail me. I am a million broken pieces shattered in the dark. I am lost to myself.

I grope for some coherence, some truth. And it comes. But it is unbearable. It is the banal truth of life. The certain fact that our very existence, brings with it the equal certainty, that to us all, an end will come. We are all stripped bare by our naked raw humanity. To live is to die. And his time is nigh.

Fear stalks me constantly from behind. I am catapulted forward, searching for some certain beauty. But this new terrain is barren. I am thwarted, driven mad by a search for something that no longer exists. My old self. My old life. My blissful ignorance of this storm of pain. I am face to face with Grief and Death. Smug comrades in arms, lurking around together. So let me introduce you to my new friends. They are *always* greeting new people.

Hashtag
Karenlee Thompson

I have been silent for too long
My soft tresses pulled taut
in a bun of compliance;
complicit?
My lashes devoid of the black
that might suggest flirtation
or flippancy
A life of not dancing,
not smiling too loudly
of skirts lengthened
of thighs held tight
and heels demure

I have been silent for too long
My voice a soft modulation
in a knot of modesty;
moderated?
My lobes devoid of the glitter
that might suggest flashiness
or frivolity
A life of not laughing widely
or shining brightly
of blouses buttoned tight
of hidden hips
and lips nude.

When I might have raged
or whispered names,
shouted pain, cried oceans,
I slipped beneath the surface
and hugged my silence

I did not give myself
I did not consent
I have been silent for too long
Now my pain is a hashtag
and still, I cannot

#

The little ones
Christine Kearney

At 12 weeks, I go for the scan at the UN clinic in Dili. The doctor tells me that the foetus is not fully formed and that I will miscarry soon. As I stand to leave, I thank her and immediately after, I don't know why I've done this. Perhaps I want her to think that I'm coping. Perhaps I'm embarrassed by the fact that this doctor who I've just met has had to tell me that my pregnancy will end. Perhaps I feel a failure.

Perhaps I don't know what to make of this, of the very guts of life and death going on inside me, happening to me but somehow without my full comprehension.

A year later, we have a small ceremony for the baby in the cemetery above Maliana town, my husband's hometown.

Amá, my mother-in-law, and Aunty Joana have been at me about it. Where did I put it? Aunty Joana asks. By that she means the largest clot, the bud which might have become a baby. I flushed it down the toilet I think but don't say. You didn't keep it? she persists. No, I didn't.

Ever practical, they decide that a ceremony should be held none-the-less.

'The little ones can be spiteful,' Amá says. 'They can cause no end of trouble for a mother if they're not laid to rest.'

Maliana cemetery sits on a hill above the town and the lush, broad Maliana plain. In the crowded section of the cemetery where other family members are buried, there is a wide, short concrete grave, painted blue and with a row of small concrete crosses above it. The word ANZU, angel, had been etched into the grave long ago. This is where other babies, other angels, are buried.

While our two girls play among the headstones and my husband and relatives tend other graves, Amá, Aunty Joana and myself gather beside the angels' grave. Aunty Joana lights a candle and fixes it into the earth. She says some prayers and makes an offering of a few coins.

She buries a small square of blue cloth, decorated with tiny yellow flowers. She addresses the child. 'You rest in peace now,' she says firmly. 'Don't go bothering the mother.'

Then we turn our backs on the candle, still burning on the ground, pile into the car and sweep back down the hill into town.

Only later will I feel that something I hadn't even known was awry has been put to rest. Still, sometimes I think of him, of her. They hover at the periphery of my consciousness, this life that was ours for a time, then not, in me for a time then gone.

You rest in peace now. A good angel, a fleeting angel, mine, not mine. We marked your place with the other angels, beside a small blue concrete grave, on a hill looking out over the town and the lush, broad Maliana plain.

I Have the Weight of a Life that is Substantive and Real on my Shoulders
Sook Samsara

Grieving begins when the person whose death will vibrate through you is still alive and ringing. It begins on a lunch break when you can't make it across town to visit them and get back to work in time to earn your twenty dollars an hour. It begins on a morning where everything is going wrong and you promise you'll go later to that wing that smells like disinfectant and is titled after some missionary who died so long ago even the marble is forgetting their name but you end up not having time and there will never be a good time to stand on that threshold with sweaty hands looking in on darkness that is now within one you love too.

Grief grows behind your turned back like a child until it's so big and ugly you don't even recognise it as yours.

You can't grieve publicly; you must grieve in the privacy of your own home lest your grief contaminate passers-by and the whole world gets infected with grief and calls in sick and nothing gets done and the world stops turning from the black force of our grief and we realise that the war that will finally destroy civilisation will not be fought on the sea or in trenches but in the secrecy of the heart, a long and lonely war that has been waged approximately forever.

Most of all you must pretend your grief doesn't exist like a hefty bill you haven't opened yet.

How come the sun can find time to travel 150 million kilometres each day to celebrate and grieve for itself and you can't even drive across town to hold her hand, old and thin as the Salvation Army fabrics she wears? You can't find time to go tell her it'll be alright even though you both know it won't. And maybe she won't even be conscious, maybe you'll pop over and she'll be asleep and you'll promise to come back and never come back.

Your mind turns on what she sees and must be thinking every time she wakes up in that strange room she will die in and suddenly there's tears on your steering wheel and you're shaking and you think you're having a heart attack and maybe you'll die, maybe you'll die before her and you'll never have to go back to that facility that makes your soul feel like it's a small pool of water under a heat light, but you're not dying, grief has just dawned over your planet, and you pick up the phone and call in sick and finally go see her and on that day she can give up fighting, and on that day she dies graciously right after you leave, she waits for your footsteps to echo out the building, the last conversation she'll ever have is just her consoling you, and the tears never end because they were there from the start and the sky is clear and on that day she dies.

Knitting, Endings and Grieving
Anne Boyd

He was dying.

With two nurses in the family, we'd managed to care for him at home, administering oxygen and analgesics which had inevitably graduated to Morphine injections. He was in the terminal stage of his cancer and I was digging deep to find words to comfort him.

My relationship with my father had never been an easy one – no show of feelings had been his life scripting. This was the weekend I had volunteered to stay with him while my stepmother had a break, and I could see that words were not the main issue.

I had brought my knitting. Strangely, it was a sweater for him, using much of my collection of wool endings in improvised stripes. The soft clicking of the needles broke the silence and I at least found it soothing. Perhaps he did as well, for he opened his eyes every now and then and peered at what was developing as something of a rainbow spectrum.

As I reached the finish of a row and especially if it was time to change wools, I snipped the end and tied it to the new colour, and in turn peered at my father to see if he was still alive. And so we passed the time, the precious little left of time, his time passing, his life slipping by, diminishing as the sweater was increasing.

There was an irony in that I was knitting a sweater he would never wear, yet it was the medium by which we seemed to be communicating in those last hours. It was the focus of our acceptance, our contentment and our grieving. I was knitting as if my life depended on it. Knitting the warp for the weft, weaving together the life shared with my father, and the life not shared.

Tying up the loose ends of unfinished conversations, misunderstandings, hurt feelings.

And now, peace and contentment reigned as he lay dying, and then died. I sat for a few moments more, knitting to the end of the row – the finish of the jumper. After the funeral, I tied off the endings.

These days, whenever I feel a bit down, and when I am alone, I wear the jumper and remember my father. I am grieving, but it is somehow cathartic and I again feel the peace and contentment of that ending of his life.

A hard won Spring
Tahra Baulch

But first, the Winter that Death came calling. We hadn't met before which might be why I didn't recognise her and so duly let her in. Perhaps her visit was long overdue. Considering.

At first she was an unobtrusive guest. She kept her distance and was very quiet. Occasionally though I'd hear her singing softly. I couldn't catch the words but the melody intrigued me.

I don't think the others noticed her. Sitting in the corner there. Watching at the window. Lying in our brimming bath. Sometimes I'd refer to her obliquely, perhaps hum her tune a little. But nothing seemed to rouse recognition.

Once though someone asked me roughly 'Do you have Death staying with you?' An anger ripple rose. A sense of cornering. She seemed so benign and besides I'd grown accustomed to her company. 'Of course not' I lied. And that was that.

A year passed with her gentle lingering. The seasons came and went which in itself was bittersweet. Time trod on regardless. Regardless time trod on.

But then I approached. It was on a short dark day when the winds were howling. After a vicious night.

My arms wouldn't lift to wash my hair or to pour some tea. My legs couldn't bear the weight of clothes or gravity. My eyes twitched. Jaw cracked. Pain ricocheted. Muscles mocked. My addled mind was full of fog and longing for forgetting.

I just wanted to ask about her song.

She sang it for me. Nestled in my room. On the floor with the curtains curling and grey clouds looming. She sang a whisper song of release. Promises of sleep. Resting long and deep. As soothing as a lullaby. A final sweet relief.

But then I heard our car returning. Little legs running down the hall and three bursts of everything tumbled in. One suddenly on my lap. One so loud about so much and the other smooching at my sodden cheek.

He soon followed with his eyes full of 'how are you faring' and a coffee in his hand. 'We brought you this just in case'. He crouched down to me, he bent down, he reached those arms of all there is around my fractured frame. And we sat, the five of us, and watched the storm roll heavy past our window. I let them hold me. I finally let them see.

And I was one of the lucky ones. I know that to my aching bones. For the siren song of suicide finally let me be, after a battle hidden warriors know too well. And I recognise her voice now so will try not to sing along. But that Winter was bitter and far, far too long.

Sometimes, Love Isn't Enough
Louisa Simmonds

You looked the same as your sister on the scan; a moving blob with two legs, two arms and an over-sized head, floating in the clear waters of expectation. When the sonographer joked about your 'undercarriage,' we knew you were a boy. I wasn't looking for anything else; your illness was invisible back then. There was no sign of the crossed wires and chemical imbalance in that dancing body that lit up the screen.

We made plans and assumptions. We hoped you would have your dad's brain, his perfect nose and his talent for hitting a ball. Secretly, I hoped you'd get my creativity, my thick hair and my passion for the arts. You would be your sister's best friend.

Your talent for music was a surprise; especially when Dad is tone deaf and the only tune I can play on piano is *When The Saints Go Marching In*. And I didn't want to curb your creativity but the way those lyrics grew in your brain with the ferocity of cancer (and were later inscribed on your arms), was obviously the first real sign. I was proud of your overwhelming sensitivity to injustice as well, until you directed it at us.

We assumed that if we loved you and did right by you, you would love us back in the same unconditional way. Like for like. But something I should have known is that living life isn't a process that necessarily works to plan; not everyone gets a fair go. Sometimes, love simply isn't enough.

We should have known that we couldn't protect you from the ugliness of your peers; nor could we force them to accept you. We should have identified that by accepting your anger, we were doing you a disservice. The posh word for that is 'enabling,' the psych told us, which roughly translated means that we weren't helping you by loving you that much.

We weren't the great parents we assumed we would be at the scan.

I still can't explain what happened to that innocent fetus that waved at us from the screen, or the perfect life we had mapped out for him? When did the cheeky grin disappear and the laughing green eyes fill with hollow inkiness? Where did that obsessive desire to puncture the fabric of society come from?

My heart aches when I see you now, when I know that it should be overflowing with love and pride - a mother's pride. I hate the way your dad struggles to make eye contact with you, or how much that hurts you. I hate the way I trip over my words when friends ask about you, and how the dog and your sister flinch whenever they hear your key in the door.

I became that mother who could throw her son out of his home and then bathe for days in her own tears. Tell me what else I could have done?

Tell me why love wasn't enough?

Fells

Philip Radmall

After my brother's funeral, I drive north across England
looking for crag tops and ridge lines and high scrub; for steeps
lifted out of catchments; for the juts and brunts of an old earth
set firm in its exposed face and inward thoughts. That if there is to be
a telling out of this, a lore to guide me now, it will be riddled
through some stark fell side, looming and dour and obdurate,
baulked up blunt and hard to the meek give of sky beyond.
Like I should show to it my own ground, the great shifted mass
of being brotherless, the sudden upthrust and tear through heart
and matter so I am pushed and sundered, broken away and recast
like a new world formed, bleak and alone and left with it all trying to settle.

As I step out and climb into these hills, the sense of them deepening
further from their base, they are damp with the last day's rain, bog-marked
underfoot and scored with run-off, until they steepen quickly into
open slope and moor and stand out barren and scoured, bearing visible
their years, above a valley left slunk in its vast down-width and reach,
and all around is heady with distance and awe, sheer and leaning
and unfamiliar, as I press another foot down and trust to it for all that.
Now I am high out of harm from him, from his gaunt form
sunk in the low bed which, if I caught or touched, cried out
with pain from him that crippled me to the chair where I sat watching
the inertia of each heaved breath's thin clutch and catch and groan.
Too late for talk or questions, only the set image of his slow leaving,
in the half-dark of the small room's last grasp of him, where the stiff
bone-racked body stayed and pulsed for its own sake still.

So I huddle against a boulder's anchoring on the flat gorse and the scree,
on a hill-face made resolute by weather, welted by winds and tested
by the lengthenings and shortenings of millions of days, its ground stolid
and unflinched and coping, as I watch the late mist coming and the heights
of these fells closing into their own introspection, and the light
softening against it all, and press to the lichen cold and wait for instruction.

Black News
Anthony Levin

It comes without warning. Black news crackling through
the blue husk of day. My physical whereabouts shrinking
with the light in a violet smear. The phone pressed against
my ear like a shell, your voice dragging hushed tidal potential.
Suddenly, I'm the night-swimmer who does not see the wave.
When it topples I collapse, my voice warbling like a lost calf.
On the sea-grassy bottom, I lie in a heap the shape of despair,
my black bag slung like a deep-sea creature latched to its prey.
Only some of your words break through the black: *Metastases*
and other deadly sounds. *Metastases* ringing in the depths.
Down here, Echo does not reconcile. She listens to the stones
of the years dropping at intervals like some broken xylophone
sinking towards the ocean bed. There in silted slumber you in
your bed cast a fossil's spell. The beginning of my deathless love.
Nine long months. I witness bedside the slow-motion collision
between your body and a word: bones standing in for bonded
glass and alloys, filling and buckling one by one. Unseen *metastases*
slipping along the marrow run. Secreted in its hissing breath,
the slow sound of your death. And you lobbing predictions
about your date of departure – as if it could be booked. But
it turns out you were right: the date arrives and you begin
your leave with the hollow, whistling tune of a broken flute.
I listen carefully to your *platzenmusik*, holding my breath
in the space between the notes, bringing my ear closer to
the silence. A memory of you returns like the ghost of a river
retracing its path over long-dry earth: You, justly centre-stage
amongst your tango coterie of Italians, Egyptians and Jordanians,
sharing a joke; until your laughter becomes our deathless love.

a black point

Niko Campbell-Ellis

The last time I looked at this view I was a different person living in a different universe. I can't comprehend the bitter world I now inhabit.

This place has always been a turning point for me, a punctuation mark. Black Point. An ominous name, the black point in my life. Maybe it's a full stop. I could do it today. Perhaps.

The first time I came here, the sun was shining and your father piggybacked me over thistles to a hidden patch of grass. We lay on our backs watching clouds shapeshift, gradually shedding our clothes. I always believed you were conceived on that bright afternoon. Your life beginning to an orchestra of waves and gulls.

Time after time I've come here again, to face into the wind and make a choice. Sometimes, when you were a tiny baby and I didn't know if I could stay another day with your father, I'd walk up here with you strapped to my chest and we would breathe the salt air together. I'd climb through the railing, sit on the black rocks and look down into the churning water. I'd thrash it out, talking to you, my speechless confidant, in a monologue of misery and regret and what ifs.

The last time I was here feels like so long ago. A lifetime ago. The wind bit and snatched our condensed breath. You weren't even sick then and the cold didn't bother you. You skipped along the boardwalk, red scarf flapping. I showed you how to climb through the rail and stand where it was safe but scary. You gripped my hand and breathed fast but then you let go. Oh my daughter, you were so brave. You threw pebbles off the edge and we watched them disappear into the foaming waves.

Sitting beside your bed in the hospital, I sometimes thought of this place. Black Point, so far removed from all that sterile white. Did you think of it too? Did you want to be here? Should I have carried you away from the clean and the machines? Away from the well-meaning but hopeless people? Should I have carried you, so light by then, to this place? Did you want to breathe this air one last time, smell the salt, hear again the orchestra you've known since the beginning?

Did I do wrong to let you die in that white place, under those lights, with tubes and needles invading your frail body?

I don't know if I will survive this. I've heard people say you should never have to bury your own child. But as I let the gritty ashes slip through my fingers I wonder, what of casting them into the salty wind? What of pitching them into the air as gulls keen and the ocean batters their pebbles to sand? And what of not knowing if every choice was the wrong one?

Bendalong
Michele Seminara

in memoriam B.G.T.

I wish when you
came to the cabin that morning
I'd stopped rushing and asked,
Would you like some tea?
and taken the time
to sit down with you at the long table.

It would have been fine,
just to trade idle trifles
and benignly swell our day —

You taught me how to fold
in the middle, ducking deep
down into the chill rock pool
to explore the unplumbed world below

before leading me back
through the rising tide, scouting
a safe path to tread.

Now I hope someone shows
you how to fold in the middle;
I hope someone guides you
where to place your feet.

I hope someone helps you
to sink, without strain,
to the glittering floor of your mind.

First season
Jane Gibian

Mountain air, the toasted-brown scent
of pine carpeting indistinct tracks,
their rounded edges softening back
into wildness. For us to discover
the creamy knots of orchids blooming
in secluded corners of the unstructured garden
that spirals out around the carved gravestone,
pine needles thickening in drifts at its base.

Finely shaped handle smoothed through
years, the Berndorf rostfrei butter knife
is a slim fish, tail still twitching in my lined
hand. Perfection of the teaspoon,
an elongated mouthful; red and white china
from a country that no longer exists.

Wattlebirds sleek and dappled
in the budding foliage: our first season
without you. The lyrebird vanishes round
a shady bend and a scattering of bees
pause in the glade of ixias, open mouths
angled in unison towards the sun.

A Japanese Airman Forewarns His Wife

for Tetsuo & Asako Tanifuji
B.R. Dionysius

*Do you desire earnestly/wish/do not wish
to be involved in kamikaze attacks?*

We are the last divine wind exhaled
from the Emperor's bleeding mouth.

Human instrumentality; my wife perches
behind me in the cockpit, her hair in a bun.

The engine whines like a dog that's missed
its master for some months, lost then found.

Aluminium coffined; we are together again.
I bring my mother no joy; we married young.

The clubs are finished bruising my face. I
have my fighting spirit, Asako has my back.

There are ten of the squadron left; we took
an oath under orders that there will be none.

Asako's voice gibbers like a ghost, she is scared.
I tell her how proud she makes her husband, 22.

*In the event of poor weather conditions when
you cannot locate the target, or under other adverse*

*circumstances, you may decide to return to base.
Don't be discouraged. Do not waste your life lightly.*

The T-34s are factory fresh & glint in
the bloodshot light. They stretch for eons.

Our pledge is stronger than a star's gravity,
just one piece would fall through the centre

of the earth. It is time to dive. The sun &
my wife urge me on. We all bank as one.

We lived by a few days to see the atomic dawn.
Nothing we do is futile, everything has an end.

Our plane is obsolete. The tank rises like a steel glove.
Asako's chin rests on my neck, as we burn with love.

Grieve

You know the measure of your love by the weight of your loss

Enjoying Grieve Volume 6?

Get all previous volumes of Grieve in eBook and paperback from the Grieve Project website:

www.grieveproject.org

Visit the site for sample works, to download your free copy of our *Best of Grieve* anthology and to order all previous volumes.

chemo days
Trisha Pender

so many little deaths you cannot possibly count them
this is not *la petite mort* of pleasure, beloved of poets
this is chemical warfare, conducted with poison
every three weeks you will find me here, hooked
to something like a giant gin distillery only
the special's high vis orange and the bartenders
all wear masks. Still, this is a social place. If you are not
puking into a bag you can join the happy hour. I get
dressed up for chemo days, by which I mean I make
an effort, when I can. I like to look as if I don't belong,
like I wandered in by accident and stayed cos it was fun
I'm too young for all of this they say, but what age
would be right? my frailer elders do not come
with use-by dates – they do not burn to shuffle off
their mortal skins, so far as I can see. They chafe
like me against curtailed expectations, depleted
daily joys, the broken bell curve
of the chronically ill
                        what I miss most is hard to name
a future, sure, that's easy, that one's big. it's more
that I don't know how long I have with those I love
Should we, for instance, go on holiday?
Or – if time is short – would it make sense to stay
at home, to burrow in like wombats, leave the world
well lost for love? I worry how they'll hurt when
I am gone and should I make a start selecting
recipes for my wake?
                                and then there's
lesser woes: the lack of tastebuds, hair, sensation
in my feet. small when singular but each erosion
of integrity adds a layer to this loss, a new graft
to the grief, a cumulative shortfall
in the currency of hope

Cairo
Natalie Holder

I fought to name you

Your great grandparents had met there, and I thought it was romantic. I imagined the way the letters would look on paper and how easily you would write them with a crayon in your hand.

The day they told us you were nonverbal was the same day your older brother sang 'you are my sunshine' for the first time and I thought of the movie *Rain Man* and wondered whether you would one day compose, and he would sing.

It turned out you didn't like sound. Some children have nut allergies and the teachers send notes home saying - Absolutely No Peanut Butter. I considered putting an Absolutely No Noise sign on our front door and leaflets in the neighbours' letterboxes *Can You All Be Silent*   (Please)

Your great aunt insisted she lay hands on you. She spoke in tongues which scared me and then rubbed oil on your chest *Will you castrate him when he is older?*   *He is NOT a dog* I said.

I took you to Brisbane for Applied Behaviour. You stayed awake for five entire days and nights until I was so tired my teeth hurt. During the flight home you reached for me. That feeling of your little brown fingers clutching mine is as precious as your birth wrist bands.

We sold our house on *Trade Me* and used the money for something new, someplace not measured by the things you couldn't do. For a while life was quiet. You were quiet too.

I watched you try and capture dust as it shone through our leadlight window. You danced flipping and flapping your arms to an imagined beat. *I was lucky to be chosen* I told people who said *they were sorry.*   *It must be so so hard* they said. Then I got morning sickness and you smeared faeces into the grooves of our wooden floorboards. There was no respite in *blessed*.

Someone from the behaviour team came to help us. She dunked gingernuts in earl grey tea while I modified your behaviour myself. In the paperwork that followed her clumsy wording read: *It was inhumane to grow rose thorns on the top of the fence, so he wouldn't climb over it.* Did she have any humane suggestions to offer? None in the report she sent.

When you turned fifteen we bought you two *Thomas the Tank Engine* DVDs. You watched them over and over, over and over. Over and over and over again. The Teacher's Aide thought we should get you something more age appropriate. A couple of days later, your father found you in our para pool doing stuff to an enormous blow up seal. He chose to laugh - *it is age appropriate,* he said.

    I have your only kindy painting. The colours of the world you see. In the left-hand corner

    Cairo

    The letters formed
                    by me.

No-one is ever really gone

Tim Hardy

I was diagnosed with Bipolar Disorder in 2013 after almost giving up on the fight which I did not know I was fighting. I openly tell you this to help reduce the stigma that still surrounds mental health.

In the years that followed my dear friends own suicide, my own mental health deteriorated to the extent that I tried to take my own life in 2013. Soon madness had worn me down. It's easier to do what it says than argue. In this way, it takes over your mind. You no longer know where it ends and you begin. You believe anything it says. You do what it tells you, no matter how extreme or absurd. If it says you're worthless, you agree. You plead for it to stop. You promise to behave. You are on your knees before it, and it laughs.

It wasn't until my good friend who now I call a brother, ran 15km and kicked down a door to break into my house and save my life. At this point I finally admitted I was sick. Driving to the hospital in the back of an ambulance asking myself how it got this bad. The horrible realization that I just tried to end my life.

Soon after my bipolar diagnosis arrived and I started to get the help I needed. I still till this day continue to fight this disorder.

Suicide can be difficult to understand for anyone who hasn't entertained suicidal thoughts.

Some people consider suicide a selfish act. I once thought this to after a close friend ended his life.. This is not the case. The decision to end one's life is often due to what people perceive as a lack of choice, the person who takes their own life believes it is the only way to stop the pain.

If I ever get to that place again, I'm determined to open up.

I'll try and explain what takes a person to the point where they cannot conceive of living any more. Despite having seen at first hand the devastation wrought by the suicide of a loved one, I was at the point where I genuinely believed that everyone who knew me would be better off if I wasn't here anymore. All insight and rationale is lost. It's not necessarily that you wanted to die you just don't want to carry on living. There is just an unending blackness in your mind, which you think will never end. In turn you became very good at hiding it, putting on a mask.

When some clarity starts to return, you can't quite believe you nearly put everyone you love through such a horrendous ordeal. I won't in the future. I'm in the best place I can be at the moment, busy equipping myself with the tools to keep on top of my illness. But if I ever get to that place again, I'm determined to open up to those around me before it's too late.

There should be no stigma in talking about suicide

Blue

Karen Wickman-Woldhuis

She died on a Saturday. The last day of Spring. It started as a day not unlike any other Saturday. I didn't make it in time, none of us did, except her nurse. The nurse said she ate all her breakfast for the first time, for the last time. The last supper. The last breakfast. The last. They dressed her in white. I'd never seen her all in white. Birth, marriage, death; white. A life laid out in white. White noise in my silent mind. No sound. No words. I had no words.

I had waited for death and now it had come. I had waited for years, through the pain, through her pain and mine. Now the day was here. That long awaited day. Today. The sky was a brilliant blue. Not a cloud in the sky. The cloud was inside me. I was the cloud. Where is the rain? The grey? The wind? Oh, to feel the wind on my face. To feel. Surely it would help to feel? To grieve? To cry? To feel something, anything.

I had no words. None that I could say. How do I say them? I had said them in my head. They had tumbled over and over in my head and then there were none. I tried, but the words stopped on my tongue. The words from my heart were lost, caught in my throat on the way to my lips. Blocked. Silence. Pain. No words. Empty words. Empty faces. Empty.

How can I grieve? Don't think. Don't feel. Don't grieve. Don't. Her death is her release, not mine. Her blessing, not mine. Years of pain, finished with breakfast. Now the pain was mine. My silent scream is deafening. Will she hear if I cry? No tears she said. 'Don't grieve for me.' No? No. Tomorrow is the start of Summer; for others. A lifetime of Winter is mine. In my heart, forever Winter.

She died on a Saturday. That Saturday of a remarkable blue, cloudless sky and a white gown. Unfamiliar white now clothed the beautiful empty shell of her body that once held immeasurable love, hopes and dreams. It now held my unspoken words, a lifetime of memories and a flood of tears. My mother. My beautiful mother. My true compass. My word keeper. Mine.

Broken
Decima Wraxall

mother shouts cheater
i cover my ears
against the clamour

the front door slams
it shakes our father loose
i don't understand . . . shushed

if i dare speak his name
or ask why he's gone
in the awful silence

of night i crave his stories
he'd tuck me up in bed
forever since i saw him

christmas day daddy's on our step—
love his grin armful of gifts my brother
sister and i rip paper crackle strip whoop

mine's red shiny and just what
i wanted i tug at his sleeve
begging him to stay mother pushes

me aside flings our toys
into the street go
and never come back

i choke throat ache
my eyes burn and sting
but boys don't cry

long after dark
with everyone asleep
i creep outside

and hug my broken train

Those Days

Sarah Bourne

There were days when I wished you were dead; those days when I couldn't carry you another step further although you were straining to see the ducks on the pond. Those days when I couldn't lift you into the bath, those days you either wouldn't eat or wouldn't stop eating. Those days when a friend might drop in and say,

'You need to get out, I'll look after her,' but I knew you'd cry and moan and fret if I left, so I didn't.

'Thanks, but we're fine as we are,' I'd reply, and watch them walk back to their perfect lives, relieved of any feeling of responsibility – they'd offered, after all, hadn't they?

Those days when you lay in your bed writhing in pain that I had no idea how to manage, how to ease. Those days when you yelled but formed no words that I could understand, so I didn't know what you wanted and was left feeling helpless, hopeless, guilty.

Those days when I felt so alone, so responsible, so afraid.

The days I wished you were dead I usually ended up wishing I were too. How could we go on, we two? You getting bigger, more aggressive, less able. Me getting older, slower, weaker.

The days I felt like I couldn't go on, I knew I had to stay alive for you and sometimes I hated you for it.

I know I am a burden. I can't do anything for myself. My limbs are stiff and crooked, my mouth won't form words. I dribble. I pee and shit myself. I did not ask to be like this, but I carry on because of your love, because without me you would have nothing.

I wish that I could tell you of my dreams; to be able to walk next to you and hold your hand, to ask you questions about the animals and the flowers we see on our walks. I'd ask why people smile at you thinly and look away quickly – is it my fault? Is it pity in their eyes, or their own grief? They don't even look at me. I am too 'unfortunate' to be seen.

I want to tell you I love you, and I try, but it comes out as a strange sound, half sob, half moan.

These days, these empty days, I sift through pictures of you and an ache starts in my ribcage and spreads to my heart and lungs so that I can't breathe. I double over and clutch myself, holding in the sadness, the anger, the guilt. And sometimes a rumble starts in my belly and builds to a crescendo in my throat and I shriek and yell and rock.

There were days when I wanted to you be dead, but I never wanted you to die. And now there is a crooked space in my life where you should be.

Debt for Life
Barbara Rosie

'Grief is the price we pay for love'

She runs her fingertips over the embossed letters on the Sympathy card picked at random from the memory box balanced on her thighs. It was a tradition now, this reading of cards on the anniversary of his death; a reminder that she wasn't the only one who had mourned his passing. But after all this time she was the only one still paying that price.

When had it started, she wondered, this relentless ache of the heart?

Not at his funeral, where the treacherous sun had streamed through the stained-glass window of the chapel to cast a rainbow shroud over his coffin, mocking her private agony. Where the collective grief of friends and family had merged with hers to become a palpable thing that bowed her shoulders with the weight of it.

Not on the morning he died, either, as she sat hunched at the side of their bed, listening to the space extend between his breaths. Watching as the colour drained from his face; the absence of life making it impossible to mistake death for even the deepest of sleeps. He was finally at peace, and yet she was filled with an almost unbearable sorrow and a dread of being alone in this new silence. No, she had been accustomed to the anguish well before that – even before the treatments had ended and there was nothing more to be done but keep him comfortable. The beginning of the end. She had lost count of the nights she had fallen asleep on pillows dampened by tears that never saw the light of day.

So when had that cold tendril of grief snaked around her throat and began its gentle constriction? The first day in the oncologist's office perhaps, when the goose bumps stood up on her flesh and she had to clench her teeth to stop them chattering, even though it was nearly forty degrees outside. She had stared at the doctor's mouth as he spoke, desperately trying to read his lips to help understand the words that seemed to be coming from some distance away. Her husband's hand found hers and held tight, his reassuring warmth focussing her concentration long enough to hear the words she had been dreading.

Twelve months.

We have one year.

Her world had tilted on its axis and when it righted their hopes and dreams had shattered and it was like searching for the future through a kaleidoscope. Yes, her chest had hurt from that day forward, like a shard of broken glass had pierced her heart.

And yet here she was, ten years later, still missing him in her own quiet way; that exquisite pain now dulled to an ache as familiar as breathing. But that was the way of grief wasn't it? The deeper the love, the greater the price. Forty years plus interest. No regrets; she would pay until they were reunited once again.

A tea-rose for Frieda, *Deutsche Shäferhund*
Louise Wakeling

I peel layers: white gift-bag   kitsch brown box patterned
like Christmas and tied with a brown ribbon   and inside
a vacuum-sealed bag with the cloud-grey dust
              of your too-brief life

fur-tufts still blow across the gravel path   the green rubber ball
rests near the fountain like a good intention   your shade
patrols the fence-line to spook the neighbour's chickens

In your last weeks I'd step into the night with torch-glare
stare down stars that dwarfed me – your eyes flickering
on and off like glow-worms – haul you back again
from darkness to a warm soft bed

Ferlinghetti says   dogs are realists
wiser than me   you were trying to let go
hung back when I reached for you
drifting into shadow   a ghost already
melting away to your favourite plot
under the lilac tree   that spot
where you'd lie, alive, among fallen leaves
turning the clivea to mush with your big body
your big invaded body

but here are candles and a perfect pink camellia
in a bowl   the neighbour's gift   a bi-coloured tea-rose
for your black-and-tan   *Baronne Edmonde von Rothschilde*
hunkers down for winter in the garden bed you dug up
in your frenzy   hunting forgotten bones   scattering the path
        with soil and mulch

all in all   your demands were small but insistent   you'd have ruled
the roost if I'd let you   I cursed you often   but find it fitting
that you're scattered here   your passion come full circle
in the promise of a wildly-perfumed rose

I wish I knew

Helen Angela Taylor

Your patient file stated that my birth was routine. I disagree.

When I was born you gave me away to complete strangers. Government calls it adoption. Psychologists call it abandonment. I don't have a name for it even though it's the canvas upon which my whole life has been painted.

People said you gave me away so I could have a better life. Better than what? I wish I knew.

When I was thirteen Mum told me she wasn't my Mum. Well, not my 'real' Mum. I said, what does that mean? She said, it means you're special. But I felt different. Other. Odd.

For eighteen years I wondered about you. What you looked like. Where you lived. Why you didn't want me. Whether you wondered about me, too. I searched for you in the crowd at the local shops, and on the train platform on the way to school.

When I was thirty-one we met for the first time in a seedy hotel on the city fringe. I brought flowers, and a heart begging for belonging. You brought a pile of loose photos from your past. Some black and white, some colour. Faces of people I'd never met. We parted without touching. Not even a hug. I phoned the next day to thank you. You didn't return my call. I don't know why. I wish I knew.

When I was forty we met again in a noisy nursing home in the western suburbs. You shared a tiny room with a skeletal woman who kept crying out for cigarettes. You looked different. Mellow. You wanted to know all about me, you had many questions. But it was hard to talk in that cramped room with the crazy lady in the next bed.

You said sorry. You cried. You sobbed. I held your hand. I held back my tears. Until you said I was beautiful.

When I was forty-four you died. The brother I've never met buried you next to the sister I've never met. He tried to find me so I could attend your funeral. Even posted an ad in the paper seeking me out. I didn't see the ad. I don't know why. I wish I knew.

I wish I knew you.

Custard
Lindsay Watson

My grandfather died begging for death. Choking on years of work down in unforgiving mines, because safety measures were nothing more than a canary. He was in pain. He couldn't breathe. Death was a welcome release from it.

I didn't see any of that.

I saw him in his last lucid moments, where he was refusing treatment, and I sat at the edge of his bed feeding him cheese sandwiches and custard. He smiled and told me how much he loved me.

I told him I'd see him again soon.

I chose not to go back the next day. I'd spent a week the year before at a dying grandparent's side and didn't have the strength to do it again. I chose instead to wait for the inevitable 2am phone call. The one I knew was coming when I walked out of the hospital.

I respected his wish to die. His refusal of treatment would only prolong the miserable existence he'd been forced into in his last weeks. Forcibly removed from his home by well meaning people. Well meaning people always do things forcibly.

The panic started that week.

The funeral sped towards me with light speed. Too fast for me to register everything that was happening. To handle the conflicting emotions about what I was feeling. About my grandfather, both a bastard and someone who loved me. The people, who chose to see him as nothing more than a bastard.

I still have conflicted feelings about that.

The panic.

When it's at its worst, it's unbearable. My body turns traitor against me and all my focus is hijacked, and I only know the sensations that run through me. My therapist calls it an arousal response but I don't like that. Arousal doesn't describe the unwillingness I feel in those moments. The fear.

Fear that I'm not having a panic attack, that I'm actually having a heart attack. That the pain in my chest isn't my heart beating too fast, it's my heart stopping. Never to restart. Every breath I struggle to take is my last. The tears running down my cheeks will be dry by the time anyone finds me.

It never is. But each time it happens, that's the sensation. There's a finality to it and I lose sense of myself. I lose myself.

Dropped down a hole, too dark to see the bottom. I stop recognising the face in the mirror. I stop recognising me. The panic swells and I try convince myself of who I am. Of the person I'm meant to be.

But I don't know who I am. So I frantically convince myself that I am the person other people believe me to be. I anchor myself to that. To the people in my life. They're the lifeline in these situations. Without them I am adrift in my own nihility, unable to form a whole.

With you, when I listen to you, absorb you, you become an anchor.
xx

Ashes
Gillian Telford

Allihies, County Cork

The rain melts the frost as she wipes
a space clear on misted glass, looks down
over drystone walls to Ballydonegan Bay
and out, way out to the Atlantic.

Beneath Knockgour Mountain, houses pin-prick
the landscape or hug the ridges, crouched
against the wind. This is where her mother
was born; a place she'd never thought to see.

And it had seemed there was nothing left
to say, that what had passed between them
before her mother's death, was over.
But here, the land is insistent—sward,

cliffs, wind; her half-closed lids
forced apart to watch the clouds mass
low in the sky, to listen—
and let the country speak of her mother.

The rain holds off then falls again
even as words catch deep in her throat.
On the quartz-crushed beach, waves sift
and drag, the tailings as white as fallen snow.

If she'd known— she would have saved ashes.

burial
Connor Weightman

a week after arriving in canb with L, the one night screening essential blood moon
spectacular, mum messages to say there's been some really sad news out of margs
. with shocked static all over the broadcast it's hard to see anything through the
wind
shield. for a few days i'm not really sure where to put it or what to do with
it. i know it's there, much like consensus suspects dark matter as the end
of an equation, a ubiquitous absence difficult to hold or draw on a map. i try
coaxing it out with curated songs, but here i get stuck on the performative
(i am also the audience at the time). i ask mum if i should fly back for
memorial but she defaults on policy: it will be really incredibly sad, she reiterates,
as
though this is a reason not to go, so i sit and let it sit with me, assume

/ hope eventually it will erode on its own
like notable limestone off victoria's coast or a kidney stone, and by one measure
he isn't clockwork, but a demonstration of half-life pinching
every, sometimes, occasional, scarcely, til each renewed blip seems
like an errant fantasy i've conjured. i no longer tell L that i feel sad; go back to
unpacking, working. there's the inevitable slip of his timbre or wry anecdote
creased at access, repeated over-retrieval from narrowing stacks
or quietly obscured by accumulating shrapnel of
it, while, it
denatures to embedded historical curiosity. after just a couple
months in the capital, L clears me out, informs: you are keeping
too much hidden at present to be baseline relatable. and now inter
state talking to a friend about what isn't in line two hitches me back to
three elderly relatives in one early year   , still i attended no funerals,
not missing school, where strangely i also remember once boasting
about not crying while dad learned of his mother's on the phone. jump
to when my cousin   and having to pretend the cause
, that everything   was basically fine because afterlife is just
divine, and at least then i could anger at the eclipsing of it, it, it,   yet

here i'm struck by rolling images of: when the cat went, sleeping on the lawn
while i was away. or parents taking the family dog to be   telling us
after. or at a hospital with mum hearing my great-nanna's voice
it . or how i'll have to tell my parents about L
but. like a movie where the protagonist never appears on camera
or measuring the lip of a crater not   to know the centre, surrounded
by the extraordinary bread   th of   the orbit s   of

Motherless Daughter
M. Fletcher

I have a new purple dress reclaimed from the second hand clothes box at the religious organisation that would be my new home. My small hand traces over the callouses on my father's work worn fingers, hoping to distract myself from the shiny wooden casket which they tell me holds the body of my mother. Everyone around me is singing 'What a Friend we have in Jesus'. A single tear falls onto my cheek telling me that I must be feeling something, sadness, despair, abandonment, loneliness but my eleven year old self could not distinguish these emotions amidst the overwhelming isolation that I felt. I think to myself my Mum is in that box and I will never smell her again, or see her face, or feel her arms around me. These thoughts try to break through the icy numbness inside.

My father takes me into a small room just big enough to hold a piano and a single lounge. He tells me that my mother is 'gone'. Gone where? Such is the language to describe a person's demise as though you might call up a curse if you spoke the word 'dead'. 'You will live with your brother now because I cannot take care of you'. This small room would be my sleeping place for the next few years but of course in this moment I could scarcely understand the enormity of my loss.

I creep, weeping, onto the bed where my mother lies in that twilight between consciousness and unconsciousness. She woke in the early hours 'delirious' my father said. He left her in my care while he delivered keys to his workplace. She opens her eyes and says 'I'll be alright sweetheart' and then drifts away from me. She does not speak to me again.

These are the fragments of memory that frame the death of my mother. My sixty year old self tries to fill in the gaps by seeking information from siblings who were adults at that time. But, their own grief obscures the details of her illness and death and their foreheads furrow trying to remember the details of those awful days.

Her death divides my life into before and after. Before, a family home chaotic, sometimes violent characterised by neglect but a place where I belonged somehow. After, a strange landscape where I wandered seeking a place to be fully myself. Motherless daughters seem to be always seeking that woman who would love and accept them simply because they had grown beneath her heart.

Ultrasound
Lisa Jacobson

There is the fullness of fertility, and after,
The egg-crammed womb — it doesn't consider a time
resounding with the emptiness of its own making.
The technician's cold instrument probes the last polyp clinging
like a leaf to a tree.
All seasons have their turning.
Loss can be beautiful.
Growing old is like tending to the house of your body,
like sweeping dead leaves from a path that unfurls,
somehow, into a future you didn't see coming,
fertile with the brutality of longing.

Circumference of desire
Jenny Pollak

I

I haven't mourned you yet.
Not properly.

The way you say goodbye when a body is buried
or scattered.

I remember your limbs.
The way you held them so precisely

the light was like embalming fluid.
I went crazy with photographs.

The light on your branches
a kind of zen poetry I tried to capture

in zeros and ones.

Though all I could catch was the equation
desire left on my retina.

II

The shopping bag the crematorium gives you puts death
in perspective.

I want to make my own bon-fire
in the dark of your root balls.

From the very beginning you committed your life
to one patch of earth.

I didn't know then the sea was a mouth.
I thought you'd outlive me.

Time was a forest your body made.
I slept in the shadow of your hands as they wheeled past.

For two decades
I lived without clocks.

It wasn't an illusion I saw the face of god
in how you apprehended the sun. Every day

aligning your needles in perfect chlorophyll
halos of white fire.

As if it was the most natural thing to do.
As if you had a secret arrangement with Pi.

Residue: a small amount of something that remains after the main part has gone
Judy Mullen

I watched him lining up the shoes like soldiers and tucking the laces inside them. The brushes, rags and tin of black Nugget were arranged neatly on a sheet of newspaper. It was his after-work ritual. Water the garden - hose in one hand, cigarette in the other – then polish our school shoes.

I wanted to do it as well as him.

'A decent amount of polish on your brush', he said. 'Firm strokes. Don't pat it on.'

I tucked my hand into a shoe and copied him; ch-ch-ch brushstrokes against the leather until a dull sheen covered scuff marks and kicked toes. Then he picked up the rag. This was the magic bit. He rubbed until the dullness became a glossy, black, liquorice shine.

'That's it,' he encouraged me, my skinny arms rubbing until they ached, 'put a bit of elbow grease into it'.

'How's that Dad?'

'Check your rag,' he said. 'When there's no residue, you're finished.'

It was the same with everything Dad did. Chamoising the car, manicuring the lawn, arranging his tool-shed, organising his finances. Preparing to die. Always thorough and meticulous. 'If a job's worth doing …' he'd said so often that we'd chant back 'it's worth doing well!'

The night before he went into his blackness, I tilted him out of the Smokey Dawson recliner. We had the routine down pat. His hands on my shoulders, my arms under his, steadying his toothpick frame. 'Now, up and lean forward.' I gasped at his featherweight. 'Alright, 'round we go.' Chest-to-chest, we began the turn-around shuffle, backing him into his wheelchair. He stopped mid-turn and I felt the faint tap of his heart against mine. He smiled. 'We're dancing' he said. My laugh took me by surprise. I looked into his fading eyes, 'Yes Dad, we're dancing.'

His last dance. Our last hug. His last words to me.

What was the point of it? What the hell was his life all about? 62 years, and then nothing. Where did you go Dad? I couldn't find him. I couldn't hear him. I couldn't hold him and feel his heart beating against my chest. Where are you?

Finding him took a long time. He appeared first in the face of my small son – the same eye problem, the glasses. Then when my husband held our daughter on his lap and called her his 'little princess'. I heard him before I left for work on rainy days 'You'll need your storm stick today.' I smelt him, when Mum cooked lamb's fry and bacon. Dad was everywhere. 'Remember how he'd let us have a sip of his beer?' my brothers laughed. 'That's Grandpa,' I told my kids as they studied the photo, 'at my wedding. Dancing with me.'

Eventually, I found Dad even closer. 'Great job,' said my boss. 'Thorough. Meticulous.'

'Well, if a job's worth doing . . .' I said.

When there's no residue, you're finished.

Camp David
Thérèse Murphy

I was wearing a neck to ankle evening gown. Blue satin at midday. Mascara streaming down my face. Thirty-eight degrees as we staggered, slipped and tripped our way up a hot, sandy, hill-track. Carrying the Ashes of David through a brine-licked scrub - the love of his life by my side.

'Scatter my ashes in the water' he'd said (waving imperiously from his Palliative bed)

'From that clifftop near the village where I once ran as a Sandy-Grommet-Child'.

(He was off his face on morphine at the time- but I knew where he meant).

That lighthouse - above those scaly columns of rock - near the basalt that had squatted in hexagons for millions of years (ever since the sea had slapped the lava stationary).

I was dressed up because he would have wanted it.

He'd hassled me for years for wearing Ugg boots in public.

I was driving my best mate – his husband. We parked in the wrong carpark and heard someone say:

'She's blowin' 45 knots maaaate'.

The 'maaaaaate' was snatched out of his mouth and whipped south.

Fuck, it was all too fast.

They'd just returned from their twenty eighth anniversary in Paris.

Still made each other laugh.

Every. Single. Day.

David left the building one week before the Aussie Gay Marriage Thingy was passed…(not that they cared about a wedding) - but the lack of legal 'recognition' meant that his love – his Husband of Forever - was left with nothing.

All went to his sister (and the sneering, disapproving family).

The House, the Art, the Lot.

Hitting a low-hanging branch I was snapped from my reverie when I smacked my forehead.

Hard.

A purple bruise in the mirror next morning - where my third eye is supposed to be.

So, we teetered our way to the clifftop. The rabid water below was hurling frothy whitecap invectives at the shore.

Like some Slow-Mo-B-Grade movie we began to scatter his chalky dust.

Two Urns; Big bloke. Big heart. Larger than life.

Dolphins leapt, sea-eagles circled. Wind changed direction. (Yeah, I said B-Grade).

We got covered in it.

In your face bitches!

How appropriate, David.

We three of the gallows' humour.

I looked at his not-yet-husband . . . his not-ever-husband, and without thinking, to the tune of that: *Little Bit of Monica* song . . . I sang:

'A little bit of David in my ear, a little bit of David in your beard, a little bit of David on my arm'.

We laughed. We cried.

Assaulted by life. Salt water below us. Salt water inside us.

Salt water down our faces.

Camp David?

We miss you every, single, day.

Circumspection
Paul Hetherington

1.
Words don't take us far, in this hospital room where age encroaches like disease; or in recollection's bumpy weather, where days and weeks compress into bunched years; or under summer's childish incandescence. You're circumspect and in retreat, and I handle your words delicately, feeling their dryness, like a moth's papery wing. Yet the river we remember is glossy, as if someone had polished glass—you lean forwards and I see myself in your swimming gaze. Now there are never sufficient words—our pauses are grief's main failure. I want to speak with our previous mouths.

2.
My moth-like father floats through a heath's mist; through absence so viscous it holds my arms down. I notice dark flowers the size of eyes; feel the room's furniture clinging to breathing. My own shape is vague as the heath stretches into distance; as a horse and cart bounce across a damaged track. The driver nods and I see the disposition of a familiar mouth. But this room presses me; chairs and tables hamper my legs. The visitation is the mind's eddy of currents and thermals.

Custodian

Norm Neill

That night, alone,
I wept cold ashes
in a tiny silver box, a gift
from friends in Amsterdam,
and locked them safely
in the beechwood cabinet
beside the stairs.

The hallmark corresponds
precisely
(forty years ago)
and every Sunday afternoon
I take the casket,
sit beside an unlit fire
and hold it silently.

Each March
I polish the silver,
raise the lid
to reassure myself that everything
is as it might have been,
and read again
Yeats' *Reconciliation*.

Soon I'll die
and someone will come
to clear the house
where he or she will find
the little casket,
lift the lid and wonder,
possibly aloud,
why anyone would lock away
an empty box.

Dear Diary
Richard West

My dad is dying.

The doctors thought he would die yesterday. They said the same thing the day before. 'It's close,' a nurse said today, 'it's close.'

'Thirty days,' the senior consultant had said a month ago, 'Maybe a little more, perhaps a little less.'

My face had telegraphed confusion and shock.

'You appreciate this is an estimate,' said the consultant, concerned perhaps I might mark a date in my diary.

'Yes, I appreciate that', I said, not appreciating anything at all.

'We cannot predict the timing of such events. There are too many factors to consider.' He hesitated and then re-qualified his thoughts, 'but barring major developments I believe your father's expectancy will fall within those parameters.'

'I understand,' I said, but I didn't and couldn't.

Neither did mum.

Today is Day 28.

Mum punctuated our hospital visits with her need to escape for a cigarette or three. She sometimes did this legally, by walking outside, or she did it illegally and locked herself into a toilet where we could hear her sobs and smell the smoke. The nurses looked the other way. And Mum stayed out of jail.

I looked at dad's old army photo I'd stuck on the wall behind his bed. I did this on Day 5. Every doctor, nurse, carer and cleaner commented on his Hollywood good looks.

My dad had been an athlete, a gymnast, a champion swimmer, a motorcyclist, a dare-devil risk taker. The photo and the dying man were as similar as hope and despair.

Dad stopped recognising us ten days ago. Now he slept and woke in a muddled mess of morphine and confusion. Tubes pumped liquid life into him; tubes channelled liquid waste out of him. In. Out. In. Out.

Each day saw more pain; each day he received more morphine. It was a 'two-man race' for the winner's ribbon. Neck and neck. But in the last week the morphine was streaking ahead, leaving pain behind as the sorry loser. But the 'loser' took dad's brain with him.

Dribble oozed from his mouth in a snail stream beaded with bubbles, sometimes a weak pop would punctuate the silence. His body was closing in on itself like a crab claw clutching to a shrinking morsel of life.

In neat cursive the photo above his bed read: Johnnie (Germany - August 1949). It was his birthday. Dad was twenty, a radio operator in the occupational army of a defeated land. He stared at me from the photo. A young dashing man that didn't smoke or drink. But the former vice would soon suck him into the addiction that would kill him. Forty a day, every day. A habit he and Mum shared. But Dad only dabbled in drink. Mum was an addict of both. So far, she had not smuggled miniatures into the toilets along with her ciggies.

Day 29: Dad died.

Mum followed dad four years later.

I miss them still even now I'm older than they were.

4pm
Sara Crane

Brown skin big hands that beat up time
like my favourite boots imprinted and too stubborn to break
you carried me foot by foot.

Mulga and leather somewhere on the Mehi
threading bait for my delicate hands that fall into waiting mouths
like the jigsaw embers that float down from our camp fire
hot tea black, was your calling card.

Where sky and river are the map that gets you home
your mum ran down the street when you came home from war
already met by industry men a job
you chose the Man who was less mean and went working on the railways.

Guilt, sounds like a pop song
Where you die alone like the soldier you were
death
is the afternoon sun and a cup of rum.

We
were not of words but work
stashing away what we rightfully took
small places, we own
arthritis took you by the time you could buy a dinghy
you left the Mehi for me.

The day before you died you ticked the yes box so gays could marry
95 years old a man of your time
you called me up because you couldn't walk to the post office box
we had no funeral just a wake
with a rainbow cake and plenty of rum.

I sleep like a mosaic
and stack memories like tiles
the exits close me in
but in Central station I am never alone

a man on smoko, takes a tea bag from a nail and dunks it in his tin cup.

Loss sits like picket fences,
but death
is the afternoon sun and a cup of rum.

A Letter
Anahata Giri

Dear Corrina,

Memories of us drift through me. Remember when I showed you how to draw love hearts, huge, in red crayon - all over the wall? Remember the bedroom we shared - your half a sprawling, creative mess, my half neat. Sometimes, there was a line of socks down the middle if we had a fight.

Once we put our hands on our hips, and scolded Dad for being so mean. We were brave in the face of Dad's violence. Growing up, I really needed you, my feisty younger sister.

Feisty, but you also had this mellow, glowing presence. We were teenagers when I first told you

'You are like the moon.' 'Yeah sure' was your scornful response. But I would say it to you, over the decades, 'You are like the moon.'

We were teenagers when we raged against the Patriarch. We shared the pain, we left Dad and then we shared the liberation. I was 16, you were 14. Oh, the freedom, the rising above

and into our 20s. We became activists. We protested, consciousness raised and empowered ourselves to act to save the world's rainforests. I remember our daring.

Every three weeks, in wetsuits we swam out on surfboards to blockade the next huge ship carrying rainforest timber from Malaysia. We cringed a bit to tell Mum about arrests, fasting, jail, er, Pentridge in fact, but then would laugh at her predictable response: 'Whatever you need to do dear, just be careful.' Then the Builders Workers Industrial Union put a ban on the use of rainforest timber on all Victorian constructions sites! Woo hoo! We were changing the world.

Then our 30s. You follow your love of the Spanish language and move to Argentina for ten years.

You become a lioness mother. You, so gutsy, you had a home birth in your small flat in Buenos Aires with your husband and - whoops - no midwife.

You return to Australia and we enter our 40s.

You did not want to spoil Christmas day so you told us on Boxing day. The diagnosis: stage 4 breast cancer. Cancer became the backdrop for the next three and a half years.

I love the photo of us, taken eleven days before you died, aged 45. It's a real 'sisters photo' — you with your knockout smile and I see, once again, that you are still like the moon, radiant.

In the hospital, we cried over your biggest heartbreak: leaving behind your twelve year old daughter.

Then back at home, you moved into the calm.

The day before you died, you said to the palliative care nurse 'It won't be long now.' With your usual practicality, your almost fierce competence, you got on with it. You let dying move you on.

The calmness of your dying, the fullness of your living, the radiance of you, a gift that breaks my heart but mends it too.

Grief still has me drawing love hearts, for the shining moon of you.

Love always,

your sister.

Choosing
Gail Hennessy

I heard a young woman
on ABC radio, her voice mellow

cadenced with concern for her
clients who come with plans of

colour and texture to stitch memory
into fabric to reflect their love of life.

It's an unusual occupation
making clothes for the dead

I imagine they must be old for only
the elderly embrace inevitability.

2.
I remember the day we went shopping
to buy you a dress for your birthday

I remember the tilt of your head
as you turned to look over your shoulder

your reflection in the dressing-room mirror
the way the skirt fell, a swirl of pleats unfolding

while the other dress captured your hips
slim fitting navy silk, you always loved navy

we couldn't decide so we bought both

plus a thin gold leather belt
like a ribbon of honey

then we chose shoes, soft leather sandals
pinkish beige, elegant, strappy, frivolous . . .

3.
After we had decided on flowers
my brother said, you must choose

something Mum liked to wear

the two dresses side by side in your wardrobe
the sandals still paired in their box

and

the choosing too hard on my own.

Comfort
Steve Evans

What can be darker than midnight
Except midnight without you,
A few minutes before the first new day
That does not have you in it?
Shops will open.
Traffic will stream to daily offices,
There will be songs that you won't hear.
The purr of your voice still in my ear,
Before it drifts to the next room,
Then fades, seldom heard.

I will forget your touch,
Your hand on my face.
But when I remark, unguarded,
On a swallow's flight
As if you are here,
You will be back, or have never left,
And I will be unprepared for your company,
The terrifying comfort of it.

Ether

Jo Withers

I recorded that movie that you love.

I finally washed your clothes from the bottom of the basket and folded them neatly in your drawer.

I finished the book you were reading on your bedside table.

I still travel past the pub on Friday afternoons although I know you'll never need a lift home.

I still write to you. I tell you how your lilies are growing and your grand-children. I need to feel we're still connected, that things aren't moving forward without you.

Sometimes, it helps. Sometimes, it makes things worse.

Sometimes I would give anything to have you back. Other times, I want things to stay as they are. If you came back, I'd be terrified of losing you again.

Friends are despairing, losing patience. They try to fill the gaps, distressed by my inertia. Sometimes, I force myself to smile so they feel better.

I live in the ether now. I am a half-being, with no place in your world or theirs. I live on memories and lost moments. I feel that I am vanishing, as though I walk through the world unseen.

I dare not step sideways and allow the present to encompass me or your memory will fade.

I feel guilty when I laugh or my concentration slips to reality for a moment.

As time rolls forward it gets harder to remember. Every day I repeat small details in my head so I don't forget. I recite them over and over, like a prayer.

I will keep you alive inside me. In the ether I still hold your hand.

Lost

Jacqueline Damen

If you asked me about my identity, I am not sure what I can say. Who am I anymore? Am I even me? I don't have hobbies. Hell, I haven't read a book, or exercised, in months.

The only time I am free is when the baby is sleeping. I haul my broken body off the couch, make a cup of tea, and trawl mindlessly through Facebook, then Instagram, then Twitter. Without even realising, I am back to the first after the third. Life with my baby is wonderful, but life for *me* is a loop of no motivation and post-natal anxiety.

For three years I worked in a job that I love, teaching. On a contract for those years, always with the promise of an ongoing opportunity – 'one day'. I work so hard, with love for my students and passion for the craft. With a baby in my belly, I go for yet another ongoing job. I am, once again 'pipped at the post' I am told, by someone else with decades more experience than me. But if he weren't there, oh yes, definitely the job would have been mine. This job was my last chance. I leave for maternity leave – but is it really leave if there is no full time work to return to?

I feel unwanted, but the students think *I* have abandoned *them*.

Sometimes I meet with ex-colleagues. They marvel at how sweet my child is, and how wonderful they are sure my life is. Having a break from teaching, yes, it is nice. They ask me kindly, what am I up to, how's life?

I have no news, but I mumble something about an online course I've started. My baby starts screaming down the cafe. I have to go.

Who am I without my career? I often stare at the Occupation field on forms for a long time, and wonder whether I can write 'teacher'. I no longer have a workplace; I no longer have that community. I rarely speak to adults – so when I do I often feel that what I say is irrelevant, banal.

I hear that due to a change in the enterprise agreement, all teachers at my school who are non-ongoing have been made permanent. I have missed out because I am at home breast-feeding my baby. My principal calls me to get some photos of an event I ran, and feigns exasperation at the situation. If only you were physically here, she says, working, we could have kept you.

A colleague texts me in March: had I heard that a student had died? No, I had not. I do a Google search and see that the funeral was three weeks ago. I cannot pay my respects, I feel so far from where I was. He was one of my favourites.

My sadness is deep and I am very alone. I sit on the lounge room floor crying, my baby clawing at my top.

Eulogy
Grace Dwyer

My favourite picture book, my grandfather's cushion -
were incinerated while workers in the crematorium
burnt him, who now lies in a timber cabinet
in our living room, next to a bottle of Hennesey Cognac.
Once he went missing for hours
and we found him later in a box
with Gumption and Windex when the removalists went home.
When he was 16, education was spelt J-O-B,
his studies laid the foundations for someone else's future -
his diploma was a building licence, his mortarboard yellow.
He wanted to be a writer like his older brother,
but no one has his pages, or knew his characters
on a first name basis, so I can't tell you about them,
but I do know that somewhere
between eating all the sweets he wasn't supposed to,
and hiding from his wife, he taught me make-believe,
reaching for the insulin syringe, I was a nurse,
tending to his condition. He bruised like apples
stacked in the wheelbarrow shaped fruitbowl
of my childhood, slow healing cuts
were lines of red texta from colouring books,
his tiredness an excuse to take naps
with me each afternoon. Sometimes
I get a craving for oranges cut on the back
of newspaper, specifically the sports section,
which neither of us cared for. He preferred reading
to me in the backyard in front of the Muscats, or listening
to me play my mother's school violin.
I did not know the notes,
and strings were missing, but he managed
to make his clapping echo, like an audience
of thousands.

In black and white
Ian Wicks

It's only now, at this distance,
with grief's long shadow at last receding
that I'm beginning to see you, in black and white.
Behind that stern face, captured in a rare photograph
before Sunday church, there must have been a broad country grin
to win Mum's gentle heart, yet I have no memory of it.

I'm looking back at the sixties, and a grainy composition
of Commission houses, lining a treeless suburban street,
to our bare front yard - where you look awkward
dressed in suit and tie, and much older than thirty-five.
Your right arm rests on my shoulder, protectively;
your left hand holds my younger sister close.
Oh Dad, what you were thinking in that moment
captured by the open aperture -
was it just country diffidence,
or were you already restless, already careworn?
Not long after, you were dead and gone
and we were fractured by grief
in a blink.

Much later, we learnt that as a boy
you played the violin at your bush convent school.
We never heard you play –
some antidote it would have been
to hear real arpeggios ring
above that soulless suburb.

We have so few photographs.
I wish there was just one of you
holding a violin between shoulder and chin,
elbow and wrist framing correct angles,
bow balanced gently below the bridge,
your gaze composed
on its phantom strings.

Blue
Deb Godley

Your face I remember best
The low-slung smile
My eyes lost in the silken wrinkles time gave you.
My little hands on your cheeks
Staring into your soft eyes
Grey.
Tiny nose on your nose.

You smelled of kerosene
Rose powder
Cigarettes and dripping
You were sunshine
Yellow.
Your hands, your cough.

Grandfather grumbled under
Angry caterpillar eyebrows and a shiny dome
A smoky haze orbiting
Like the ashtray on his table.
Brown.
I tried on his leg while he slept and you laughed

You taught me about Jesus
The Queen and the Tarot
Avon perfumed princesses and leprechauns during
Long baths that made me wrinkled too.
White.
You built me a crown of bubbles.

You left me after my wedding day
A tiny perfect flower
Perfumed with rose powder and kerosene
They all said you wore the wrong dress but I knew
Your favourite colour was
BLUE.

Everything I need to know (letter from a widow)
Susan Bradley Smith

Dear Robert Lowell (Cal),

The London sky this afternoon is alcoholic—golden and dangerous. My husband died on such a glorious day, this time last year. Like you, his death involved public transport, and a mistress. You died in a taxi that had driven you from JFK Airport to West 67th Street, just off Central Park. You were returning from Ireland, having just left your third wife, off to visit your second. Tell me, how do hearts feel about being attacked? And do taxi drivers take the rest of the day off after such an incident or do they not bother? Cal, you hard-drinking glorioso, you monster, you emperor, you tyrant—why were you clutching so furiously in your arms that painting of your wife? Your dead-man's limbs had to be forcibly broken to wrest that stringed, brown-papered, jetsetting parcel from your grip. Needs must. I'm looking at her now, your last wife (subject, model, muse, marrier of mad painters and poets): 'Girl in Bed' by Lucien Freud. The National Gallery is hung with secrets, they swallow them, they declare them lacunar, nail them to walls of varnished vernix, keeping them alive, if silent. *I will eat you for breakfast, drink you for dinner, kill you for bedtime,* says the girl in the painting. If I was that girl, if I had been Lady Caroline Blackwood, I'd do it all again. I know. I'd do everything again, from the sable to the hogshair to the sawn-off arms: oh, to be held so fast, so tight, painted so bright, that is a commonwealth to die for. Meanwhile, I'm waiting for my date. I'm bothered. But my shoes—high-heeled pumps, shiny patent leather—make me happy, marking the floor with important pecks as I move from portrait to portrait. I amuse myself wondering of each: would I kiss them? All the while, though grateful for the human eyes tracing my runner's body, I can feel the onset of panic at being alone and in public, I am honey turning to comb. I am, it seems now, always alone and waiting—how must your ex-wife have felt, when you failed to arrive? Volcanic, ready to Pompeii you, I presume. God, please bless me with such geology, and memories stronger than sandstone.

PS If you could have, you would have written about your own death. It was as you'd wished, in some regards: natural, no teeth on the ground or blood about the place. Things I need to know before grief eats me alive: is that what men really want, to return to their ex-wives? Had you been kissing the painting? Does the past taste of turpentine?

PPS He has not come, my man. I am writing to you in the women's loos, in between reapplying my lipstick. I feel as cold as the marble sink beneath my grip. Is it warm where you are, in deadland? Have you met my husband?

Grieving is Overrated
Mark Bromhead

My court-appointed grief counsellor, a well-meaning but misguided individual, recommended that I write down my story. As if that would do any good. But anyway, here it is.

I attended St. Francis Xavier Marist Brothers High School for boys in Hamilton, NSW from 1970 to 1975.

The school motto was Viriliter Age, a Latin phrase that translates as 'to act manfully.'

I have often wondered over the years whether I lived up to our noble school motto. Consequently, I created a checklist to determine exactly how manfully I acted for those six years of high school. You might have attended the same school but, more than likely, you did not. No problem. Just imagine yourself as a student and go through the checklist. You might be surprised at the results.

In the following checklist I have used as an example one of the Christian Brothers known intimately to me and others who attended the school in the same time period. Let's call him Brother P.

Okay, now let's begin the Viriliter Age Acting Manfully quiz. There are ten statements. For a perfect score you need to check each statement as true.

1. You never questioned why a man of God said one thing and did another.

2. You never thought to tell anyone what happened during Brother P's mathematics and religious education classes.

3. You never refused to go to Brother P's after school discussion meetings, even though you knew what would happen at those sessions.

4. You were never bothered by the vivid nightmares you dreamed every night.

5. You never resisted the sexual advances of brother P, a man of the cloth in his mid-forties, with a preference for pubescent boys.

6. You never complained when Brother P stroked, fondled, and caressed your adolescent body.

7. You never expressed your revulsion when Brother P abused himself beneath his long, flowing robes.

8. You never once considered suicide.

9. You never gagged on the holy man's manhood.

10. You never ever tried to grab the metal crucifix swinging from around Brother P's neck and shove it deep into his eyeball and then right into his reptilian brain.

Well, how did you do? Did you get the highest possible score of ten out of ten? If so, you are as actively manful as it is possible to be. No doubt your life has been as successful and meaningful as mine.

Surprisingly, my grief counsellor was not impressed by my perfect score, spouting some sort of psychobabble about denial and not realising how much I needed to grieve.

Honestly, grieving is overrated. I don't get it. Grief implies some sort of a loss. What does it have to do with me? What have I lost? I just don't get it.

Even
Richard James Allen

Even in this darkening,
even in this diminishing,
even as the fires whistle out
their last red breaths,
can we not remember how to weep?
And, warmed by our shuddering
at the campfires of our grief,
so fecund, so luminous,
spill forth our wet light?

Family portrait
Grace Dwyer

On Friday morning he revoked the claim
to his body, lying supine, his left arm thrown back
his fist closed tightly around desires
and gratitude unspoken. When you called
and told me, you whispered as if reality
could be turned to rumour, making a part of me
believe that I would find him in the dust
of unsettled shadows limboing under picture frames
in the hall. No one gave his or her condolences
to the dog despite his eyes holding a candle light vigil,
floating as he shifted to lay his head in our laps.
Your uncle joked about his dead father knowing
we would all gather here, so he left
the garage fridge empty and your grandmother
who'll spend her children's entire inheritance
hoping her husband will appear, a residual spector
in the bottom of her Royal Dolton.
Sometimes when you and I kiss it's difficult
not to think about how your body is pressed
to mine, like your hands were to his sternum
when he was already waving to you from somewhere
without a postcode, though I can't help
feel he is imprinted in the flexion lines
that appear on your knuckles
when your hands are clasped in prayer -
small eternities passed down.

Fairy Dust
Louise Baxter

Mum grew up in a small town in the West Australian Pilbara and spent most of her childhood playing in the 'fairy dust' – a blend of red dirt and blue asbestos blown in from the local mine. She loved the stuff, and it's what killed her. All those years waiting for the cancer to form, from all those days spent making castles out of carcinogens.

Grandad was the first to go, in 1974. For years he'd blitzed the mine's walls while the microscopic fibres did the same to his lungs. Every day he breathed them in and wore them like a suit, then hugged his wife and daughter with the remnants at teatime. Nanna died six years ago. Mum's day came on February 8, 2017. Fifty-five years after she first danced in the dust. Thirty-six years after she married Dad. Seven months after she was diagnosed. The only number that matters now is how many days the world has turned without her in it. That's 48.

She showed us pictures of the town, in happier times. The landscape looked like a sunburnt leg with bright-blue varicose veins taking root in the arid ground. Those same colourful specks had been inside Mum, spreading like venomous tentacles throughout her body. Eventually they swallowed her whole and took her away from us.

Family photos that once gave her joy – grainy cricket matches, black-and-white front yards – became records of poison and pain. One by one the smiling faces turned into ghosts. It's still there, the dust. The town was closed in the 1960s but the traces still blow in the wind.

When you lose a loved one, people give advice. It's what they do. Give casseroles and advice.

'Talking helps.'

'Light a candle.'

'She's in a better place.'

You're allowed to cry at the funeral but a stoic presence is always admired. A few weeks after you'll run into a neighbour at the shop.

'She's so strong,' they'll tell a friend, later.

At that same moment you'll be on the kitchen floor, crying over a tin of a tomato soup. The kind you ate as a kid, dressed with a dollop of sour cream. You'll never know how she made that salty sludge taste like love.

Grief comes in thunderous waves, pulling you down with its crushing weight. You never know which form it'll take – a lamb roast, stray threads on the carpet, the smell of seaweed on a humid day. I can't bear to see what has changed, like waking up on the other side of a mirror. My sole purpose is trying to get back to the other side. I told Mum I needed the world to stay the same. She understood. She said she'd live in our memories if she could, and now she does.

We can't go back. The world we knew has burned to the ground but its ashes are everywhere. We breathe them in every day without knowing . . . like blue clouds of fairy dust.

Farewell to Billy Duluth
Lesley Carnus

The weather, as bleak as our loss, seemed
perfect for this gathering by the oval.
Huddled in the cafe, we talked and laughed,
glad to be together but ashamed of our pleasure.

The urn was raised; our heels sank in the soak
of earth as we squelched through grass to scraps
of garden behind the grandstand. Barry, too tough
for a speech of any eloquence, mumbled some words
of love and friendship; shook a fistful of ash
around the base of the struggling grevilleas and cried.

Over in minutes, we clumped in silent groups
back to the cafe. Bill stayed behind
on the grounds where he'd lived and trained,
across from the school and the two children
who were his salvation.

A man of courage and tenderness;
he must be happy out there enjoying the day
while he listens to young voices drifting
up from the playground, celebrating life.

Not Long, My Darling
Audrey Molloy

In memoriam: Anne and Geoffrey Iddon

When I found you Sunday—awoke
to the silence of the cold hand—
I cursed my lost eyes, wanted only
to take you in; the set of your shoulders,
the knots of your hands.

I was angry, won't deny it—
not with you, but the boatman.
Out of earshot by then,
he didn't hear the fizzle of my life, extinguished.
I will while away the time 'til his return,

trace a line around the house,
fingertip to wall, map the space
in which two people built a life,
where they learned: to sit is good enough,
no need for chatter.

And so, the carer becomes the cared for.
A man must travel in style
and you will wear your Panama hat,
the one you wore last year at Cottage Point,
our diamond celebration.

There will be no one to tend me,
so I laid out the dress with violets,
the claret heels I danced in,
your hand so light on my waist.
(I dare say they will burn the lot).

They'll say we were foolish to stay.
My hands, too weak to write,
my mind too frayed. I say,
lay no blame on neighbour or child;
this is how we dreamt it, how we closed the door.

A Love Letter To My Little Sister in Prison / A List Of Things I Didn't Say Because I Was Afraid
Trixi Rosa

Sunday morning pancakes, sad eye smile, she speaks soft as morning light.

That freckle on your upper lip, that dances when you laugh
and disappears into your dimple when you cry.

Saturday morning ball, all numb fingers and awkward ankles.

I'm sorry how on visitation day at first I found it hard
to look you in the eyes.
Until I realised your eyes still cradle innocence like a child.

Roof-Rocking the neighbours, like they don't know where we live.

A child. A child in an adult prison.
You went in a child, but you'll come out a woman.
So how are you supposed to survive in a world
you didn't even get to grow up in?

Reverse hand-me-down shoes.

Is orange really the new black?
And while we're speaking of color,
how much did my white skin privilege influence
the different life pathways we were given?
If you had my white skin, would they still
sentence you as an adult at age sixteen?
If you had my white skin, would they have
stepped in to help you sooner?
Before it went this far?
Before the blood you spilt was no longer only your own?

Cold summer swims, jumping in from the old Fox Bridge.

Why didn't we hear you six months earlier, when you jumped?
Could there be louder warning bells?
Like those four storeys you fell weren't enough to say hey,

I'm really unwell?
Like those four storeys you fell weren't enough to say hey,
I'm at risk to myself and maybe to someone else?
Like those four storeys you fell weren't enough to say hey,
someone
please
help!

Video Hits break battles and Michael Jackson moves.

They said you were saved by the parked car you landed on.
Since when is hitting metal at high impact called saving?
Like simply surviving would be enough
to make you want to live again?
Like time in intensive care would suck
the intensity of despair out of your bones?
Like the want to disappear wouldn't come back to find you?

Late night games of Go-Home-Say-Home with the cuzzies down the street.

I'm sorry I didn't come back to find you when I heard.
On the other side of the world,
I was busy writing my own four stories of self-destruction.

Gentle hands with splinters, cradle the corner-store phone.

Truth is sis,
I want to scrape the blood from under your finger nails,
blame mental health system fail,
blame judicial system fail,
blame the whole damn failure of colonialism,
blame ancestral trauma,
blame systemic racism,
blame oppression,
blame disconnection from culture,
blame living below the poverty line in a "first world" country,
blame him, blame her, blame me,
blame all of us little sis, all of us,
but not you.

Some swallow blame to ease the raspy cough and choke of night. Some spit it.

That freckle on your upper lip, that dances when you laugh
and disappears into your dimple when you cry.
Mum and I haven't seen it in a really, really long time.

Release date silence.

Detritus
Joan Katherine Webster

This is a time when I float aimless in
the estuary of ages, like a blown
frail thistle-down that has come down alone
on some deep pond.
              I snag and swirl and spin
and hover, going nowhere. In these thin
constraining narrows   in between time-flown
and time-to-come
                    the edge of life has grown
land-locked.

            This is a time when I begin
to peel off particles of past about
me, like a spun-off meteor
        -dust of days no more
                my core exposed as stone.
                                          Far out
there in the social cosmos people blaze in orbit
while I, cindered, fall   in doubt
of point and purpose
             through my time and phaze.

Guilty gratitude
Christine Burrows

1.
Tremors (minor irritation). Such good luck though. The luck turned you know. Finally, it turned. Luck suddenly running like whitebait on a spring king tide.

Numbness (minor discomfort). It's a miracle really what medicine can do. And a good mindset. Halfway there with a good mindset.

Nausea (minor nuisance). It's all the medication. It's a finely choreographed pharmaceutical dance. What's a bit of nausea? It's nothing. Yeah, no, really; it's nothing.

Disbelief (what actually happened?) Did any of it happen outside of nightmare? Was it the febrile dreams of a septicaemic mind and vigilant insomnia?

Forgetting set in quickly, like winter fog, swallowing geography. Memory slipped twisting away, breaking apart the continuous flow of time. Memory edited; re-arranged. Selfies and Facebook posts become the memoir. The truth proof.

#fuckcancer #notwinning #finagerscrossed #donatelife #eternalgratitude

2.
Incense curls from a swinging golden censor. Garlands of white lilies and gardenias sprawl across the lid of a polished pale oak casket. Propped amongst the flowers, a framed photo of a grinning young man, a boy. Dark hair curling across one eye. Cream satin lines the coffin's padded inside. The tasselled ends of a blue and white scarf rest on the chest of his black suit.

(Machines were turned off. Breath slowed and stopped. Flat lines declared him gone. His family washed his face and hands with their tears. Surgical teams on stand-by went to work. Removed his organs. Swift. Dispassionate. Stitched him up again.)

A dazed father stands at the lectern; slowly unfolds a hand-written eulogy; clears his throat; smooths out creased pages with quivering fingers. A quietly weeping mother cannot speak. There are no words for her grief. A sister, a brother, eyes wide and wet, stay defiant of the truth. Will their prankster little brother push aside the coffin lid, leap out and shout 'Haha, gotcha! Sucked in, suckers!'

3.

I don't know who he or she is. So I guess. I make it up. I make it up. To make it real. To justify still breathing under the ever unfurling sky with the sticky grit of sand between my toes and ascending magpie song gracing these gifted days. As newly rich blood thumps through my veins, vigorous with platelets and iron and life. It sings again.

It sings again of joy and pain; ash and flame; a strange refrain: Lazaresque. Lazaresque. Life and death. A keening elegy: Lazaresque. Lazaresque. What cost? What debt? A complex melody: Lazaresque. Lazaresque. Oh holy bequest!

A bright young life relinquished. Extinguished by delinquent chance. Their liver, two kidneys, two lungs and a heart, made six lives renewed.

One is me. Me. With my guilty gratitude.

Super Hero
Fiona Everette

Years later, well beyond the diagnosis, you think back to the day he was born and you knew it even then. That morning when the midwife said, *'I can see his head, he has hair!'* Offering a knowing smile like she had predicted the future. You looked over at him lying on the scales, little hands fisted into balls. Serious and brave. Later we would learn that this was his talent. To white-knuckle it.

He slept all night and loved books. He never cried, you took him everywhere. To the cinema, cafés, to Venice! Our mini frequent flyer. Contentedly strapped in his stroller with his headphones, baby Wayfarers and The Beatles. Years later the scales would tip and the balance would shift. You were needed more than the other mothers. To scoop cereal, to dress, to interpret and soothe invisible miseries.

On his first birthday there was a huge celebration—your first year as parents! Fifty guests brought fifty gifts: trucks, puzzles, buckets and spades. He wanted only the smallest cup in a stack of nesting cups. You admired the skill and precision with which he sent the bucket spinning on its rim with a single flick of his pudgy wrist.

Through four house moves you box up unwanted toys. Each time you unpacked them secretly hoping he'll wake up and play cars. Mothers at playgroup complain and commiserate *'my house is a disaster zone! Lego everywhere!'* Eventually you stop going because you can't bear to hear about their children's incessant questions and their make-believe.

Then come the true warning signs. The gradual frequency with which you begin saying:

'He doesn't like that.'

'He doesn't do that.'

'He's not there yet.'

Then D Day. Diagnosis day. You don't remember much about the appointment but you do remember there was no sugar coating it.

'I'm going to go ahead and give a diagnosis of Autism.'

There was advice.

'This is a marathon, not a sprint. There will be grief. Don't burn yourself out.'

We must have sat in the car for two hours. First saying nothing, just crying. Then reading the report. Puzzling over the percentiles. Debating their accuracy. Then realising it didn't matter, it had been decided.

He starts therapy and you cannot take him on his first day. You have given birth to his brother and the caesarian scar is still raw. Months tick by and it's a blur because the baby doesn't sleep but slowly there are breakthroughs. His sentences plump, he smiles more, he sings to himself in the morning tucked up in bed. He plays peek-a-boo with his brother! Interests become talents. You realise he's not just counting. He's adding, subtracting, multiplying. Cross-referencing music lyrics with time.

We return to playgroup. The boys in Spiderman costumes play chasey, ask questions, fight and make up. But he's there, amongst it. The true Super Hero. They have imagination but he lives in the 5th dimension. He sees magic everywhere. A world of mathematics.

How it is
Alison Flett

Like an orb weaver holding fast to its vast web, the shivering lines stretched over
great distances, the pin-point ends of its delicate legs balanced and quivering
casting its dark silhouette across grass

No   no wait   not like that

Like the rain falling and falling, drop after drop gathering along thin threads of web
like strings of pearls, no, glass beads, no, tears, like tears, the weight of them so
heavy the web must snap, must break, but only sags, the tears sliding together
falling and falling, drop after drop into earth

No   no wait   not like that

Like gathering firewood in the rain, the soft impact of fat drops on your bent back
rough twigs slipping their thin daggers into your fingers, the rain like seeds
like smoke, like shrapnel, burying itself in your clothes

No   no wait   not like that

Like gum leaves as kindling, their quick crackle, unzipped heat opening out
its orange wings then crumpling back into dust and smoke
sinking and rising, to earth, to sky
the tragic theatre of fire

No   no wait   not like that

Like her shape in the doorway with the light of the house shining out around her
like her shape in the doorway with the light
like her shape just there

Like looking up from the shadow of evening towards the doorway and expecting
like looking up towards the door
like looking

No   no wait   not like that

not like that

wait

Everywhere
Jo Gardiner

I see you
rising from the Gulf of Finland
your hair streaming
all your muscles slack
and shivering.

I see you
under yellow leaves
playing a violin for coins
on the old streets of Tallin
while masked wolves watch.

I see you
standing on a bridge by a lake
in wedding clothes
trembling from too much coffee
your face white with fear.

I see you
flicker outside the window
of my darkened room
a silver leaf of light
caught on your sleeve.

I see you
frantically searching your pockets
for your room key
along the corridor
of the Hotel Insomnia.

I see you
sleeping in an alcove of azaleas
in the garden of the Six Principles of Poetry
while beside you a woman
combs nits from her lover's hair.

I see you.
Everywhere I see you
but you aren't ever
coming back are you?

Cold

Karen Lieversz

Blood spills silently, welling up around the edges of the carving knife planted deeply in my lower back. My kidneys are skewered, as if prepared for a barbeque. The edge of the knife peeks out through my stomach, gleaming silver, tinged bright red at the tip.

I hadn't seen it coming. Should have. My sister has been looking right through me for years now. Guess it makes sense that she would be the one to end my existence. An existence that has offended her, an existence she excelled at ignoring, an existence she is now snuffing out with cold efficiency.

Falling to my knees I stare up into impassive brown eyes. She says nothing as she pulls the knife free of my body. The only sound, my flesh sucking loose from the blade. I slump to the floor, trying to form the words ... 'Why?' But I know it's useless to speak them. She won't answer. She has never explained, not in a way that made sense to me. She moves to the kitchen sink, rinses the knife. Blood mixes with water, washing away. Maybe she thinks her sins will be washed away as well?

Fresh blood gurgles up through my mouth. She wipes the knife and returns it to the drawer, picks up her bag and leaves the room. Doesn't give me a second glance. I'm garbage on the floor. Soon to be nothing but landfill as the cold tendrils of death seek me out.

I wake with a start. A nightmare. Again. I roll out of bed and stumble to the bathroom. There'll be no more sleeping tonight. I stare at my reflection in the mirror, remembering those moments when anguish weighed heavily against my soul. Holding onto my father as his heart beat its last beat. Wrapping my arms around each of my three beloved dogs when their turns came to breathe their last breaths. They were the moments I thought I'd never come back from. The moments when I railed against God and life. Yet it was in those moments, those precious, inimitable moments that I learned what it is to really love.

Losing my sister, though, to the dark chasm of estrangement, is a death from which there is no escape. No healing. No love. What makes one sibling turn away from another? Shun them?

Hate? Anger? Jealousy?

I stare into weary green eyes. There are no answers. No way to fix it. At least with the dead, I can find serenity in my memories. But grieving for the living... there is no peace. No peace when I cannot forgive her for splintering our blood bond. No peace when I feel my heart grow colder. No peace as numbness slowly consumes me.

I return to bed. Wait for sleep's comfort.

Darkness beckons. Darkness . . . and cold. Down to my bones cold.

I cannot move. The bed is hard, like the kitchen floor. Ice seeps into my heart.

Encasing me.

Protecting me.

Claiming me.

Looking for Clark Gable
Alexandra Geneve

'I'm going to find him if it's the last thing I do,' she said.

Hollywood cemetery is where they all are. At least the ones we wanted to find. It was the last day before I flew on to New York and my mother back to Perth. The smog meant the pietas were covered with a light dusting of dirt. I sat under one of the larger ones and read the map to the stars. Rudolph Valentino. Douglas Fairbanks. And of course, Clark Gable. My mother had a thing for Clark Gable.

'I can't find him,' she said, standing above me. She'd been gone awhile.

'Well, it says he's here on the map. Let's have another look.' We entered the first hallway we came to.

'It's cold in here,' my mother whispered.

'You take that side, I'll take this one,' I said. 'Meet you in the middle.'

There were so many names. So many dead. The floors were black marble and they echoed my mother's footsteps down to the other end.

I turned right down one of the longer corridors. The boxes there were made from shining bronze.

'Mum?' I called. Was I the only one in here? Silly. As if my mother would leave me here.

As I turned into another hallway, admiring some roses, I saw her sitting down on the marble floor at the end. A square of sunlight breaking over her legs. I stopped for a moment, not sure what I was seeing. She had a pink rose in her hands.

'Mum,' I whispered as I got closer. 'What are you doing?'

'He's not here,' she said looking at the rose. 'And I've broken my promise,'

'What promise? What are you talking about? Mum, let me help you up.' I held out my hand but she didn't move. I looked down the long hallway and slid to the ground beside her.

'When I was a girl,' she finally said, 'my mother told me I couldn't see *Gone With the Wind* when it played at the Metro.' She smiled. 'It wasn't suitable for young ladies. It had 'scenes'. Or so we'd been told.' She looked up to face the ceiling. 'That was the thirties, of course.'

I turned to rest my head on her shoulder.

I went anyway,' she said. She was still for a moment. 'It was wonderful. We'd never seen anything like it. The world, I mean.' She sat quiet and then, 'My mother walked past the theatre as I came out. I thought she saw me.'

'Did she?' I asked.

'I never knew. All she said when I got home was that she'd changed her mind and that I could go and see it if it was really that important to me. Only not to tell Grandmother,' she winked.

'She told me to say hello to Clarke Gable. I promised I would.'

I touched my mother's hair as we sat there breathing.

In the Quiet Moments
Emma Pasinati

I think about you, in the quiet moments. You know the ones. Those last few minutes before falling asleep, when the walls come down. Or in the perfectly ordinary moments of the day; waiting at the bus stop, ordering a coffee, doing the dishes. You find your way in. Those rare moments when my mind is still and I'm not aware of my heart beating in my chest. Those are the moments you appear.

It's only ever you.

Sometimes I wonder why you come into my head like that; why you, why then, why now, in this moment. I don't mean to think about you, but I do.

Sometimes I want to tell you things, big things, little things, world-rocking, heart-stopping things. Sometimes I wish you'd just leave me be, let me live my life without wondering where you are and what you're doing, what you would say. I know what you'd say. Sometimes I know what you would say before I even have the chance to figure out what I would say. Sometimes I question whether I actually knew you at all. Maybe I just thought I did. That's the most likely scenario. Because you were there, but you weren't. Not in the capacity I wanted you to be.

Not even close.

You couldn't be the person I wanted you to be but that didn't stop you from changing my life. From taking all the things I thought I knew and turning them upside down and inside out, throwing it all out the window. You know which window I'm talking about. The one with the bird on the ledge that was really me but instead of letting me fly away you held me back and kept me safe because you knew that I had no wings. You tried to help me see that. I saw it.

You wanted to give me wings.

And now whenever I think of flying, I think of you and that ledge and I sit down and wait because I cannot fly on my own, not without thinking of you first.

But it's the thoughts that come in those quiet moments that really get me, the sneaky ones, the ones that come when I'm not expecting it.

And I wonder, do you think of me?

Indwelling
Ron Pretty

Hey, Deb, in everything I write, I find
I am still writing to you. How we sent
our poems back and forth, how too often
they weren't very good – mine at least –
sent after a night of wine and candles,
as now, knowing your kindness, how
you would feel for the ballast behind them,
how you would know the intent; & then
hearing you smile as you sent a reply
revisions would flow, & I might discover
the poem in hiding. How can I write
without your voice in my ear? Truth is,
I still hear you, see your cheeky grin, know
that in everything I write, you're here.

My Dear Son
M. Wong

Dear Son,

I'm sorry we haven't spoken for a while. I was never one to dress something up so here goes, your mother died. She was a trooper right until the end, but the cancer proved unforgiving and eventually won. I know what you thought of her even without you saying it. The appreciative glances you gave her before shovelling down your favourite spaghetti dish, the flowers you found by the river and the way you said 'really mumma?' when she embellished on one of her many stories. Too much time has passed but I still hoped you would reach out to me and be here.

Remember how you said I couldn't cook? Well I actually tried making that same spaghetti dish and followed the recipe to a T. The dish was excellent, on par with your mother's. But I couldn't shovel it down like you. I think I lost my appetite a long time ago. Along with many other things.

I know I probably shouldn't bother you with this. But sometimes it hurts. It might even hurt as much as the time you impaled your shin on the rusty nail sticking out of the fence. There was blood everywhere. Boy could you scream. We put you in a bath of Dettol. Seeing you so vulnerable, with dirty tear streaked cheeks, I wished desperately we could swap places.

Occasionally I still feel angry. But it's getting better. I shouldn't be angry at the world. But I am. You had the whole world at your feet. You were an A-student and all your school teachers said you could be anything you wanted. You made everyone laugh, even Mrs Lee with her twenty cats chuckled at your jokes. And I can't ever forget the time I was working in the countryside and you caught the train, all on your own, to deliver me lunch. I was the envy of all my colleagues and everyone said 'he's a good boy.'

Well you should know, I still think of you. Your great grandfather lost a limb once. He said he still felt it, this phantom limb, a feeling that never ebbs. It's a bit like that for me. I see your face in the sea of high school and university graduates. I see you going to work. I see you as the wonderful father you never got to be. I'm reminded of the roulette wheel of life - you, not you, you - but why did it have to be you?

Oh my son, I miss you since the day you left us. I hope you are well wherever that may be and I thank you for all our beautiful memories together. You would be fifty now if you were still living. Happy birthday my dear son.

Love Dad

Let it not be this
Jennifer Chen

Let it be anything else
And we would stand up under it
It could still be hard – but give us an option, an out
A side-gate no matter how narrow,
And I would draw the marrow out of my bones if that would assist
Wrap my kidney up as a Christmas gift,
Siphon out my hot, thick blood like soup
if it could recoup her this long winter
And sustain her for another spring.

Fling
        us deep into the throes of bankruptcy for expensive treatment
Chemo that is excruciating, nerves grating, endless nights aching,
Like crushed glass behind closed eyes
only let her survive.

Baptise
        us with your hottest fire and we would improvise.
We're fighters, we're survivors,
My grandmother crawled up a mountainside for days
In a daze without food or water to escape rape by the Japanese
My uncle swam across a flooded city with his keys in his teeth and the expertise
of a man determined to see his stranded wife.
My mum would not let the Communists take the best years of her life
And smiled through gritted her teeth to show she had been re-educated
My dad lived through the "revolution" when the schools were desecrated
And escaped through that bamboo curtain
With hope undeflated and vision unabated -
He wrote his PhD before this country had looked into Chinese eyes.

Baptise us with your hottest fire and we would improvise.
We're fighters, we're survivors,
So let it be anything else
And we would stand up under it.

But let it not be this -
A paralysed recline,
The mental rewind,
This slow decline.

Resting Bitch-Face
Thérèse Murphy

I remember that night at the pub. Vodka shots by the bar. You in your faux-stoat stole. Tossing your head in the smoke. Wild brown eyes. Laughing.

Wanting to kiss you (even though I hadn't kissed many girls before).

Your poem about that Jerk that broke your heart – *his pony boy-gym-sculpted-arms* rising up to choke him.

Wish I'd saved it.

Your breathtaking viciousness: I was the antechinus *marvelling* at a peacock.

Those jealous girls that called you: *'Bitch-Face'*.

Your mother's funeral.

Nick Cave singing *Into My Arms*. Your relief that her suffering was finally over – then WHAM Nek Minute? You were stamped with the same Dread Cancer.

Your breasts:

'They had to come off'.

You were thirty-nine, I was thirty-seven. Hadn't 'lost' anyone before.

Bitch-face?

I miss laughing at the world with you - toasting our Bog-Irish-Colonial-Roots: belting out

The Pogues with *narry* a dry eye to: *'The Fields of Athenrye'*.

Fuck chemo you spat.

Mammy had her lymph nodes 'cut' by a system she didn't question.

I've got this one you said:

Look and learn: Turmeric, hypnotism, kinesiology, past-life-regressions, acupuncture.

Healing the 'sad genome' of Irish resentment.

Oliver Cromwell.

The day you went to *Palliative* was the day your *Road-Kill-Art* was 'selected' by the 'Archibald' thing.

Driving to your exhibition –was when I got that message you had died.

A *text* message.

I immediately went to ring you - to talk about how weird that was…

Drove to that bridge near your house and drank beer in the shade (dazed by the irreverent beauty of the day). Shocked by the absence of dark skies and wild wind (which had ripped my internal weather vane from the roof in the sudden gale of your departure).

Raising my glass to the sky, I threw flowers at the river that flowed past your house.

A duck dabbled by and for a moment, honey? I came over all *'King Lear'*:

'Why should a dog (or in your case, a duck) a horse and a rat have life – and thou no breath at all?'

I could make no sense of it – so went to see *Starsky and Buddy*.

Starsky your goat. That cloven-hoofed-collaborator (who thrust his horns in ambulance doors) to stop them from taking you that very last time. One hoof reaching to touch your stretcher: a gesture of homage, farewell.

I slept next to Buddy your Blue *'Healer': King of the 'Bed-Side-Vigil: midnight-soft-paws touching: You:*

The self-proclaimed *'Fringe-Dweller'* taking solace in animals, art and the poetry that was your essential marrow.

You inhabited a space outside society – but *always* inhabited a space within me.

That dastardly acerbic charm! Till the last *(even when body-snatched by that bald-chemo-shrivelled-shadow in a hospital gown)* you maintained your infinite poise, grace and humour.

Darling Bitch-Face

The shock of your absence first dragged like a sinkhole with dark ragged edges.

Now, I glimpse your spirit - still guttering *out there* - lighting spaces of sacred chambers for a Lucky Goat, a Devoted Dog and me.

On the hottest midwinter day on record
Peter Lach-Newinsky

i.m. Barbara Sterling

Now changes carry sharper edges,
cut deeper into the thin skin
of memory. The house just visible
now among the tangle of trees
from the fire-trail hacked through
your anarchically unfenced bush.

These days another person dies
every other day. Then always air
thick with silence, sudden cool breeze
soughing leaves, that dull ache
pulling memories out of now
like an overworked midwife.

Not even sure if it is your house,
the hardwood house I helped you build,
always loved being in, so small,
so large with the sheer force
of your life poor in means, rich
in spirit, your house a creaking
wooden boat with an unrailed, death-
defying deck leaping out into that
grey-green ocean of fire-loving trees.
Into all that silent, waiting space.

My Elisa
Alexandra Geneve

That night you held his large-knuckled, dying hand in your small, life-filled one for hours and hours and never once let go. You slept upright, somehow, in that plastic and vinyl hospital chair jammed next to his bed in the tiny room overlooking the church.

I draped you in white hospital blankets and stroked your hair and paced up and down the darkened corridors throughout the night knowing he had your hand in his and your sweet rhythmic breaths near his belaboured ones.

I offered you water and food but you declined. You were worried that drinking would make you need to leave him momentarily and you couldn't let go of his hand.

Instead you talked to him of Barcelona and the architecture of Gaudi you were off to see. You spoke of dreams of sailing boats off the Croatian Coast and the Gothic spires of German minsters that you climbed to the sky to touch; the worn-down stone masonry underfoot on the endless stairs you both climbed to the tallest bell tower in the world.

You told him of all the things he had inspired in you to do and all the things you would do in his honour. You rattled on into the night, sometimes speaking out loud and sometimes in your head when you felt he could hear your thoughts through your fingertips. Whilst I massaged his toes and feet and talked of the universe and the night littered with stars, you spoke of dreams and musings and your visions for the future.

You chatted to him after he'd gone when we were waiting for the doctor to check for life. You reassured him we were there and still you didn't let go. Not until the doctor asked us to step outside and not until you reassured him again that we were only on the other side of the door.

You sat with me later that morning in the sudden torrential summer rain, the two of us in our soaking wet fluffy bed socks I had bought for the vigil; both wrapped in that same blanket under the cascade off the courtyard pergola. We didn't care if we were wet through to our underwear. No one cares what you do or how you do it in those places where death is a nightly occurrence and an oddly-welcomed stranger.

You were by my side when no one else had the strength. You were there through every step of that passing over into death. Adults three and four times your age said their goodbyes and went home to wait.

Not you. Not my Elisa.

You were nineteen years old and that night and that morning you showed me how to live.

Maracas
Trixi Pavey

I first felt the fractured air of bomb-blast in a northern mountain city of Mexico
where they paint portraits on buildings of local heroes
reminders that even though sons and daughters are forced across borders to trade candy for cap guns
heroism still lives in the heart of the people

That night we shared a single sheet-less mattress, cast into corner of a grimy tiled floor
I awoke to bomb blast shatter and machine gun laughter
my lover lullabied me back to sleep with whispers of fireworks, but morning shone daylight onto crumpled concrete
local heroes wrinkled smile lines and hopeful eyes, trying to shine through rubble

this morning my phone a machine gun . . . 6 missed calls from his mum
my lover clutches his phone as though a bomb entrusted to him
his voice nails across chalkboard scream Mi Papa?! Mi Papa?!
I take shelter behind kitchen bench, cradle coffee percolator become defibrillator I will attach to my lover's chest
he comatose from blast, deafened by scrape of nails on chalkboard
his Mi Papa become a whisper without question mark like repetition invites the words to forget their own meaning
and Mi Papa, Mi Papa will just be the sound maracas make at family weddings
when his father holds his mother in tender hip swing of 50 years' joint rhythm
50 years knowing where home is, but today he will not come home

- 106 -

She clutches phone as though a bomb entrusted to her
Her husband's voice nails across chalkboard avow his love
red rivers run rampant down valleys of time etched in his face
and the doctors say a phone call was impossible with that bullet wound to head
y las senoras in the church say it must be a miracle from god, and my lover says NO! this has nothing to do with god!
his father a local hero taught the towns children alignment and backswing

and the coffee I put to percolate won't wash the maracas out of my lover's mouth
his hands shake aftershock, ears ring evacuate, and all my training in earthquake country
never prepared me for this kind of shake and shatter
I am utterly inadequate as every airplane movie for 23 hours tells stories of father-son love
we disembark into a car where no one speaks of walls freckled with bullet holes and for sale signs

At the funeral, someone jokes that the only winner of this war is the coffin maker
that these days' funerals fall more frequent than saint's days
and I know that in Mexico a saint graces every single day of the year
but these jests of desensitized death follow suffering across continents and centuries
so I hold his words like a bomb entrusted to me
as we sing nails across chalkboard, search the rubble for our hero's hopeful eyes and smile lines
and sway to the maracas that will always play in my lover's mouth

Scenes from a Hospital
Kate Ryan

How to recall it?

Lift conversation. A woman about my age is visiting her father. He came in for a minor thing and now he is dying. Tears in her eyes.

Riding in as it is just getting light. Cold.

Conversation with Seamus late at night, his voice breaking, 'now my kidneys have packed up'.

The doctor, on the phone, young sounding, an accent, saying, 'we are very worried'.

The man sharing Seamus's room, a baker who, years ago, lost one of his hands in a bread cutting machine. Afterwards he opened a milkbar. Blood pooling around the heart. He had the same surgeon as Seamus.

Seamus saying he might sue.

Hand sanitiser making my hands dry.

Seamus shuffling, pushing a metal trolley with his lines attached to it. We thought it was routine and he would get better.

Pointing out the holes in his arms where they have put the needles in and saying water tastes awful. Taking a single spoonful of yoghurt.

Seamus hates being called mate and says that the nurses who call him this are usually rough.

But the grace of most of them.

Ilsa, who Seamus says looks like a Renaissance painting, saying 'my pleasure' when asked to change a urine bottle or a gory looking dressing. Magda, the oldest, an air of frowsy comfort, forgetting what she has come to check. 'Sorry darl!'

Mark, gentle in everything, needles, moving Seamus in bed, changing dressings. Seamus crying when he says goodbye.

Doctor, very tall, leaning over to impart bad news in the corridor to a small man about a patient. His father?

Asking for milk for Seamus's tea at the nurses' station. A plump nurse saying his meal doesn't look too bad – she must be hungry! Sliding it, untouched, into the rack of the trolley.

Buying a copy of *Goodbye Mr Chips* from the stall in the foyer but having to stop reading it because he has only a year of happiness before his wife dies.

Seamus closing his eyes and lying back.

Laurine, an old lady now sharing Seamus's room, waiting for surgery. Her granddaughter talks – about how she can't cook but how she should and about her favourite TV show and her favourite actor and her job and where she lives and how long it takes to get there. Laurine smiles with her false teeth. I want to slap that granddaughter who does not, ever, ask her anything.

Laurine tells me her daughter died thirty years ago. I see the flicker of appeal in her eyes. I just can't think of what to say. She has the TV on all day.

Laurine in her nightie, the sleeveless child-like kind with a ruffle around the neck, rubbing lotion onto her soft pale arms. This makes me want to cry.

Ilsa leaning over and drawing around the infection with a black marker to monitor how much it is spreading. It grows visibly by the hour.

Seamus gone.

memoria in aeterna

Sandie Walker

> *'when I die I want you to save my heartbones…*
> *lift them out of the ashes gently'*   Morgan Yasbincek

I took from your ashes that delicate bone of your heart formed from the fusion of our banded scars. I wear you in a brass vial, tied with black leather. You rest low on my chest, a tiny passing-bell chiming each day of two decades lost.

They cut from your body a 1935 dog licence. You wore it for how long on a greyed boot-lace around your neck? For twenty years I have worn it on a chain, disc now thinned from skin, from fingers searching for some revelation beyond the surface. Perhaps, when it has become again tabula rasa, I shall etch fresh history, and it will be then that I will forget you.

They cut from your body a silver bracelet you once took from me. I keep it near, hear in the layered depths of night your echo roll across the divide of that sharp-valley break. Should my lover's night-cries deafen me to your deep reverberation, could it be then that I will forget you?

They cut from your body thirty-five thin metal bands, each broken circle an equal measure of breath. They lay tangled upon letters and visions in your cremation box. I count them over as prayer beads, shifting symbols of years lived. When death has stretched to the even length of your life and there are no more numbers to slide, might it be then that I will forget you?

They cut from your body one length of thin red string that, like blood, binds me to you. I knotted it tight to my wrist. The colour faded, wept into veins to pulse out my heart's missing beats. The weave weakened frayed, failed, yet your love I did not forget.

Intermission

Jenny Pollak

The sea repeats itself
is a bully
is barely in control
of its own movements.
Thinks nothing
of engulfng the beach and the wharf.
The benign rocks. Last night
spilled itself
like a vomit
in cahoots with the moon.

Today the sun is dividing the body in two
parts – the neck of Palm Beach from the head
of Barrenjoey.
Cruisers and yachts fall in the gap.
The sun is so sharp I can't look.

If you were still here this would be nothing –
all your body divided
in multiple parts.
A pause between acts. With lights up
and popcorn.
Already the sun has scattered and boats
are bobbing. The sea is amiable
as a rug. It could be a picnic.
I planted your ash high above the tideline
but you won't join me.

One Lump or Two
Billie Ruth

One lump or two? No, not sugar in my coffee. Bulges protruding from the right side of my neck. More than two. A cluster travelling down my neck, egg sized lump under my armpit, a mass behind the right clavicular. One neck lump sliced and diced, Hodgkins Lymphoma, cancer, not sounding nice.

Now making sense; always early to bed, Pilates exhausting instead of refreshed. It wasn't moving house during university exams, neither the grief of my best friend's sudden death that still hovered as a dark cloud. It was an insidious curse not invited by me that was destroying my body as it pleased.

'It's not your fault, you have done nothing wrong. It is just something that happens', comforted my GP, echoed by the haematologist I now had to see. Comforted I was. It is treatable, the most curable, the outcomes are good. I just didn't know then the toll on my body and mind it would take.

The final year of my Social Work degree put on hold, replaced with appointments. Bone marrow biopsy – having a horse needle stuck into you to suck out all the goodness, medical torture. PET Scan – another needle filling you with nuclear power so you can glow in the dark for x-rays. Lung function test – that hurt blowing your guts out when you have a mass crushing your insides. ECG, ECHO test. Painless, my heart is in good shape.

Chemotherapy then radiation and all will be good. NOT! My highly sensitive body reacted to it all, rare side effects, some never heard of before. 'That's not supposed to happen' became the common response when presenting to emergency, when chemo began, when blood was taken, when with pain from an injection I couldn't walk, sit or stand.

It is nearly three years post treatment. I would love to say life has been grand. Grief and loss go hand in hand. Had no trouble losing my hair, but watching it come back curly brought despair. I would look (I still do) in the mirror at morn and not quite recognise the face that I see. A rare skin condition (thanks Bleomycin) means the sun and I are no longer friends, my physical appearance is not pretty to see, I can't wear polyester, had to change my clothes to all cotton. Miss my favourite tops. Chronic fatigue you can't see but the webbing in my couch has given way from the endless hours in front of the TV.

I have lost years. My 25 year plan blown out. Still trying to get back to university. Living on Centrelink keeps you on your knees. I am grateful for some extra financial support from family. I can tell you where all the best food bargains are, would love to have a break from counting every cent.

Life is for living, some days that is hard, when your head says 'yes' and your body 'no,' but you get up anyway and give it a go.

Since you
Beth Spencer

The new puppy has eaten one of the shoes you left by the door
and rolls with it in the dust where the old dog buried his bones

the whole universe cannot contain images enough of you
and neither can the walls or the tables, but I am trying

and there is never enough room for everything
I didn't say and didn't do and all the times (all the times)

so the clock steals sleep, its claws tick into my heart
and my darling your pillow, your pillow

I wander lost these rooms and the halls of us
tiredness like a dense fog, searching for a path back

I call to the snake under the bricks and tin in the dawn
but the snake won't oblige

and now they have velvet-handcuffed me to this life
and put me on watch

they coax me with phone calls from the little boys
with new life in the womb of our daughter, with a puppy

foot tethers! a twisting rope around my chest
the terrible pain of blood returning

and I bring flowers and put them in the crystal vase
on the table in the sea of you, in the everlasting sea

in the since, and in the sea of you

Yiayia
Sibella

My grandmother is dying.
    My grandmother isn't dying.
    My grandmother refuses all food and drink at the nursing home.
    'I'm dying,' she says to my mother in Greek.
    'She's dying,' the nurses say to my mother in English.
    'What's wrong with her?' I ask my mother over the phone.
    'She has a urinary tract infection. She is in tremendous pain.'
    I speak to my sister on the phone.
    'She's not dying.' My sister says. My sister is a doctor.
    'She's not dying.' My father says. But my sister and I both offer to fly home to see my grandmother.
    My father tells me my mother goes to the nursing home each day. My mother feeds my grandmother yoghurt, sobbing and talking in Greek.
    'I want to die,' my grandmother tells my mother in Greek.
    The nurses give my grandmother morphine.
    'Why are they giving her morphine? She hasn't got cancer.' I ask my mother from afar.
    'You don't know what pain she has. How can you be so heartless?'

My grandmother is dying.
    My grandmother isn't dying.
    'I wish she would die,' my father tells me over the phone.
    'Don't tell Mum,' I say.
    I haven't seen my grandmother for eighteen months.
    'She's old now, she's not so bad. She doesn't have the energy to be vindictive.'
    My father laughs.
    Last year we stayed at my parents' house. My mother took my daughter Helena to see my grandmother.
    'Are you okay with that?' my husband asked me.
    'I think so.'
    Yiayia lay in bed with hollow cheeks, her false teeth in a glass beside her. She stared at Helena.
    'Poor Yiayia,' said Helena.
    Later that day my mother invited the neighbour over.
    'She won't visit her grandmother.' My mother complained to the visiting neighbour.
    'Yiayia was horrible when I was a child.' I responded.

'My mother-in-law was like that. She had a wicked tongue,' the neighbour said to me.

My mother nodded. 'My mother could be bad.' She said.

Mostly to my mother, I thought.

My grandmother is dying.

My grandmother isn't dying.

My mother sits by my grandmother's bedside, crying.

'Do you want us to fly up?' I ask my mother on the phone.

'Not yet.'

'Is Yiayia dying?' Helena asks me one evening.

'I don't think so. But she is sick.' I say.

'Poor Yiayia.'

'Yes.'

'Why don't you see her?'

'Because she wasn't very nice to me when I was little.'

'Why? What did she do?'

But I can't remember.

I try. I remember feeling frightened as a child. Frightened Yiayia would explode at me. Or fight with my father. I remember Yiayia smashing a glass in a restaurant in displeasure, telling me to 'fuck off' (in Greek – did that make it okay?).

As an adult, I learned to amuse Yiayia. I became court jester to avoid her wrath.

She learned to like me.

I learned to like me, too.

My grandmother is dying.

My grandmother isn't dying.

I won't see her.

Time for Grief
Seetha Nambiar Dodd

Some telephone conversations lodge themselves in your memory and never leave. You think you hear the words 'shadow' and 'lung' and you hope the reason is the poor long-distance line and not the possibility of cancer. Your father is a smoker, after all. You pray that his body is playing a twisted trick on the x-ray machine, but your increasingly heavy heart tells you that it is probably not good news.

Stage 4 lung cancer is not good news. You begin to furiously research facts, statistics and survival rates. You wonder how long one can hold on to 5 percent hope. You realise you have already begun grieving, for life as it was before the telephone call. But this is not the time for your grief. There are questions to ask. There is compassion to show. There are spirits to lift. You lock your grief away in a safe place, to retrieve once all hope is gone.

You travel 10,000 kilometres with your 8-week-old baby because you believe that compassion transmits better through a hug and babies are exceptional at lifting spirits. Your father smiles his widest smiles for his granddaughter. You observe their mutual contentment and realise this is where you are supposed to be.

In between hospital visits, your father studies his notebooks and works through a checklist of phone calls. He notices you watching and declares that this is not the sorting out of affairs, but simply ongoing administrative tasks. You nod with false nonchalance. You wonder why you are both putting on a brave face when it is time for the masks to be lowered.

The chemotherapy works and then it doesn't. You ask the oncologist for the truth. He suggests that your sisters come home. Grief starts knocking but you do not let it in.

It is a bittersweet family Christmas. You create beautiful memories, but they are marred by the shadow of limited time.

Your sister sits by your father's feet as he dictates the terms of his funeral. She dutifully scribes instructions on the death announcement, coffin and rituals. Tears collect behind her eyes. She holds them there until she can turn away with the excuse of necessary filing. You wish for that kind of strength.

In your last few days together, you sit by your father's bed and softly read his favourite poetry. You don't know if he can hear but you hope the words of Kahlil Gibran will cut through the cancer and settle in his soul.

After the funeral, an acquaintance asks if you were close. You realise the pain in your heart is from considering not the history, but the lost potential. It doesn't matter if you were close. What matters is that now you will never be able to get any closer. Your closeness has been capped.

You travel back to Glasgow, unlock your grief and let it engulf you like the unrelenting February snow.

Not Crying, Dancing
Linda Stevenson

I can't cry, haven't cried for an eternity.
I think the last time was . . .
I can't remember.
People have asked me don't I miss him.
Well, I see some others weep,
mourn, describe their loss,
the loneliness.
And that makes me wonder
if I'm lacking, wonder what it is in me
that just forges ahead, why I am heartless,
unfruitful in lacrimosity, mistress
of plodding on regardless.

I did dance.
During those final days
home nursing
I set up the music, turning it on
first thing in the morning
beside his bed, before the feeding
and changing.
Taking his damp hand
in one of mine
I danced to the songs he liked
bringing him with me
in his imagining
round the room where he lay
stricken yet not.
A slight smile
no more words available
but the eyes, the light.
We shared. I did dance with him
right till the last day.
I did dance.

Where has my family gone?
Michael Cole

I was being bundled into the car in the middle of the night. I was only four or five years old. My mother was driving; Dad was away in the Navy. We stopped at my grandparents' house. While my grandfather was lifting me out of the car I noticed my baby brother all wrapped in a white rug lying on the front floor of the car.

'What's he doing on the floor?'

'He's alright,' my grandfather said. 'Mum's just taking him to hospital.'

He was not alright, he was dead.

When I was about six or seven I had another brother who became dead. This time I was old enough to partly work out what was going on. My brother had died of whooping cough. I can still hear some of the strange noises he made amongst the sounds of him crying.

Dead had not finished with me yet. I was twelve when my sister became the next victim of dead. She was only sixteen.

When my sister was about twelve she developed a disease called hepatitis. She was sent to the Prince of Wales Hospital for infectious diseases. The one and only time I went there I met a girl who lived in a wooden box. The box was about the size of a coffin but painted in bright colours. All you could see of the girl was her head sticking out from one end with a mirror mounted above her face, so she could see who she was talking to. This wooden box, for some reason I could never understand, was called an iron lung. Whatever was in that box kept the girl alive. She was paralysed from the neck down. She had polio.

During the war my father came in contact with TB, during years of living in close contact with other sailors in small destroyers. Infections spread quickly amongst the crew. As soon as vaccinations became available, they were given to members of naval families. When these TB injections became available for the public, every child in my school was given an injection on their shoulder. A reaction would show if that child had been infected with TB. Three days later before the mass vaccination took place it was noticed that my shoulder was bright red. The school went into immediate lock down. It was given the all clear when it was realized that I had already been vaccinated. That's what had caused the reaction.

When vaccination became available for whooping cough I was there. I was one of the first in the queue for polio. These diseases were virtually eliminated from Australia but are now making a comeback. Do those who protest against vaccinations really understand? Ask the mother of the girl who spent the rest of her life in a wooden box. Ask me, the brother of three children who died from whooping cough and other preventable diseases.

On My Mum's Passing
Belinda Paxton

Afterwards, I went walking on the beach and found
that the light was very clear and revealed
the edges of things
and shining on the sand
a feather
in its precise boat-shape
bare white and burred across
by lines like electricity.

I thought surely
this feather has come from that tender place
under the bird's wing
where she tried to save it, dear thing
pressed against the pain-riven ribs
and the organs mindlessly beating
though her breath falls ever more heavily.

It's just the way two hearts might
struggle and stutter and settle at last
for one moment of clear signal in
a life-time of white noise.

But you said there was no such thing as time
and didn't we exalt the lightning
that shattered the sky on the day you left
and showed in one blinding instant
the fractured line connecting heaven and earth?

And if you called
I still would bob across to you
on my little boat feather and
join you again in our stupid sacred struggle.

Because when you left the edges of things
gleamed and were precious
and in the refracted light I could see
for a moment
how a moment might be enough.

Renovations

Sylvia Muller

Grandma was waiting on the doorstep when my uncle and I arrived. She was older, wider and tired looking, but still the warm, gentle soul I remembered. We shared hugs at the door and went inside for lunch to the sound of the kettle boiling and the smell of fruit stewing on the stove; it was the smell of my childhood. I was comforted by the cluttered shelves, heavy with faded photographs, treasures and trinkets - exactly as they had been 30 years ago. Lunch came to the table, equal servings of sandwiches and stories about Dad – the carpenter, the story-teller, the loner and the drunk, the gambler, the guitar-player and the father, brother and son. Tales of his dilapidated house, abandoned cars and half-finished projects were washed down with tea, tears and smiles.

The three of us made our way down to the river at the bottom of the farm, taking the same path I once skipped down as a 4-year-old, my small hand lost in his. With a deep breath, I released him to the breeze and let him fall away from me. I knelt by the river's edge and reached into the water, soaking my hands in his remains. I rubbed him into my skin, and with eyes closed I saw the way he raised his eyebrows, nodding with a downturned smile when he was humouring me, the way his eyes lit up when he said, 'oh boy!' to me like I was still a child, and the frown on his face when he was concentrating. I no longer saw his aching, arthritic limp, the sad eyes, the cigarette stained builder's fingers and the alcoholic waste of dreams. Before long, all I saw was a trail of ash drifting downstream.

For seven years I'd held onto him. During the funeral I quietly promised him I'd take him home, but I wasn't prepared for weight of his remains; the kilos of cremated skin, muscle and bone stopped me from letting go. So, we sat in silence - he on the shelf and me in my sadness, for seven long years. In my grief I would take the box from the shelf and hold it close. Sometimes I would drink the night away – one sip for me, one for him. Sometimes I would talk to him, yell, blame and cry at him; but in death, as in life, he would say nothing in reply.

And now, beer in hand, I look around my house and see my father everywhere. He's in the half-finished floor boards; the pile of cladding on the veranda gathering dust, the window leaning against the loungeroom wall not yet installed. He's in the spare room, what I hoped would become a nursery, cluttered with light fittings, timber, tools, sealant, silicone and paint.

This empty house is so crowded now; filled with my father's ghost and the irony that what was once grief that he'd left my life forever was now despair that he'll never leave.

words out my mouth
Kathryn Lyster

    on that day
by the lake
at your funeral
fig tree sprawling
sky heavy overhead
squawk of cockatoos
on telegraph poles
circle of peonies
in the dirt
by our feet,
all the while
i was speaking
birds talking over
me woman opposite
staring hard like
all words out
my mouth were
the wrong kind
and i should
just shut thefuckup,
instead i kept
telling old stories
of our lost
african child hood
to the crowd
of pained faces
while soft rain
piddled on heads,
wondering how high
up you were
how many mourners
i could stack
in a ladder
and climb over
to pull you
    back to earth.

Skin and Bone
Melissa Manning

Today I am loose inside, a pocket full of nothings.

My chest is a cavern
my chest is the universe – it is outer space and the world orbits beneath my ribs
I tumble in the stratosphere, reaching
for whatever comes next – for all that was before.

Today I am a walking beast.

I move on legs that are not my own
my gut is a quagmire
a tar-pit
I am made of mercury – too heavy to be fluid and yet.

Today I am solid, inert. Useless.

I remember you hooked to wires, invaded by tubes
incessant chime of monitors
both comfort and irritant
my pretence at courage – the constant vicious churn inside.

Today I am a maelstrom, tempest; a witching manic nothing.

I think of you in pieces – in the bed, in the freezer
fragment of your skull on the shelf below hearts
I imagine opening the gates of my chest, like the impact opened your pelvis
hold my breath as if that could make a difference.

Today they say I am strong.

But I am the scant moisture
left after drought
I am the tissue-like vein of a leaf
picked of flesh.

Today I am skin on a bone frame.
Today it is the best I can do.

Some time later
PS Cottier

Little reminders of their loss
surface from below;
small pale sea-monsters,
with subtle, itchy stings.
I see a monkey statue
carved from wood
and think *Dad would have liked that.*
Or opening a single malt
I hear my teetotal mother
tut-tutting at wine or beer,
forever fearing the worst.
Grief mutates into these
quiet pricks of pain,
embroidering the day
in samplers saying
We are gone. We live on.

So I sip a whisky
and buy the monkey.
It would cavort, as monkeys do,
if it were not so solid,
carved from sheesham.
Its tail curls into a smile.
Yes, my father would have liked that.
And my mother would have hated it
when I pour a second drink.
Anxiety tinkles amongst the ice;
repeated tales of sick livers
turning skin yellow like feeble suns.

They surround me in nets
of themselves, transmuted.

Sirens
Meg McNaught

Sirens screaming, closer and closer. I still go all quiet. Reminds me of Mum. That day the ambulance slammed to a stop in front of our building.

Mum was on the couch, pale. Voice wobbly. Matty, listen, she said, press the zero button three times.

My hand shook so hard I had to do it twice. Is mummy awake? The person asked. Mum's eyes were watery, a deep line between her eyebrows.

Tell them it's my heart, Mum said, eyes pinched closed.

I held her hand. It was sweaty and cold. The person on the phone kept talking, but I couldn't listen. I watched mum's chest, up and down, up and down like a basketball was in there.

The sirens got louder and louder, the noise shaking through me. And then they stopped.

Mum told me to open the door and I stood waiting. Four flights, no lift – and Mrs Donaldson's cats in the way.

Two of them came. Serious faces, big shoulders, they walked straight in and took over. Snapping on gloves, unwinding tubes and putting them up mum's nose, thermometer in. One of them was bald with hands moving like a footballer. The other one pressed fingers on mum's wrist. Alice, are you in pain? Can you tell us what happened? The bald one noticed me, how 'bout you get mum some water. I ran to the kitchen, filled a glass, turned too quick, and dropped it. Glass shattered. Water everywhere. I froze. The bald guy, a giant, saw my bare feet. He came and lifted me like I was a skinny toothpick and carried me into the lounge and set me on the chair. Mum's eyes were closed. Dark hair long strings against her cheek. I started to cry. I didn't want to, I tried to hold it in. But big gobs of tears poured out.

Matty? Mum's voice a scratchy whisper.

I swiped at the tears, used my tee-shirt to mop my face. I'm sorry I dropped the water, I whispered back.

S'okay.

Julio and his mum came. Everyone was talking soft. Julio and I got sent outside. We sat on the steps and waited. Julio tossing a cricket ball.

On the wheelie stretcher Mum looked tiny, wrapped up tight in a white blanket. She moved the mask away from her mouth and said Julio's mum would look after me. I kissed her cheek. She smelled like a hospital.

They packed her into the back of the ambulance. Slammed the doors.

Julio behind me, telling me to come inside.

Weights tied to my legs, I couldn't move. The sirens started up. Loud and painful. I wanted to put my hands over my ears to block everything out. But I couldn't. Mum was in there. I stared at the ambulance wondering if I'd ever see her again,

Two Trees
Tanya Richmond

1.
Last night's fallen gum, waiting, blocks your path.
Push hands on her torso, split fingertips
on ragged bark clutching at ankle, calf,
thighs- her lean, long trunk and your bony hips.

Step between branches, where the easy sway
from rosellas perching and salty breeze
over the creek now is still. Yesterday,
kookaburras above called out their tease

and you looked up to this unseen soft green
treetop. You tread near light green sprigs growing
from tiny red-brown twigs, minuscule seeds
safe in their gumnuts, and bud-clusters gathering.

2.
Gnarled, twisting bottlebrush on the fenceline,
grew in the days backyards shared families.
Poison got inside, past his defense line,
Lorikeets quietened chirps to homilies.

It took one year. He shrivelled, shrank inward,
torso halved to layers of dry-mouth bark.
Grey leaves recall red brushes they adored,
one branch holds out, thick green, against the dark.

This fence he leans against was framed around
him. He watched this street get housed, then rebuilt.
Still, his weary limbs stretch far out of bounds,
and that old trunk is just now beginning to tilt.

There are days
Penny Lane

There are days I could live where trees
cluster jumble-rooted in a tangle of bush,

days I could live in an old, grizzled banksia,
coiled in fat gnarly branchings, lazing,

or nestled far up in a eucalypt, dozing
in scribbled limbs reaching into blue nothing,

days I could perch as still as a tawny frogmouth,
unseen, as much a part of a tree as a branch;

days I could lie under lichen-splattered casuarinas
for unthinking hours on a needle-soft bed,

or crouch against a melaleuca's messy drapings
and wrap myself to sleep in paperbark layers,

days I could burrow into leafen earth and wait
for the growing of wings to flutter me into the blue;

today is a day such as this,

not a day for watching my child syringed
and tube-strung to bags of chemotherapy drugs.

Vincero I will overcome.
Merran Hughes

A decade has passed and I can usually listen to Dad's CD of Pavarotti singing *Nessun Dorma* without being overwhelmed. The aria was his favourite. Dad loved to sing it *forte* under a gushing shower head at home. I press play and hum the aria. The phrases resonate inside me, amplifying my memory and making the longing clang, bell-like in my chest. Song is such a simple time-travel device! Listening, I whirl backwards.

The strings recede and I'm in the hospital after Dad's car accident. Dad has just been moved from Intensive Care, so I walk through the orthopaedic ward, looking for his bed. I hear him before I find him. He is in full flight, singing *Vincero,* his tenor rises in full *crescendo*! This thirteen-year old racket, is coming from a bathroom where Dad is being showered. I wait, enjoying his take on the aria, thinking his exuberance is incongruous with his injuries. But then again, he is happy to be alive.

The nurse is laughing as she wheels Dad back in on a bed, clean and combed. He is smiling too, at their shared joke. Dad is not aware I am visiting yet, as he cannot move his head. Dad's only view is upward, towards the heavens. His fractured vertebrae are held in place by a metal contraption, screwed into his temples. It is darkly called the halo. I didn't appreciate the humour when his entry to the next realm, had barely been staved off by the fierce team in the Intensive Care unit. They used the halo but refused the wings. I stand up to kiss him, so lucky to have a father.

'Sorry you had to look at the car,' he says. I shrug and think about the line of crushed vehicles I'd seen in the police garage that morning. The kind of place where fresh angels might hover. Business-like, I had climbed into the mangled metal that was his sedan. I had cut myself, sweeping the wind-screen glass off the seats, to salvage maps and his music collection. Including this CD, that I'm listening to thirteen years on.

Dad notices the fresh plaster on my finger. 'Did you hurt yourself out there?' He knows about that jagged steel and glass, having been pinned and cut from the vehicle. He reaches toward me, concerned. As I take his hand, the sheet falls back. I see his bruised upper arm and chest. He is as black as an eggplant. But he is only worried about me. He, with his broken neck and his pelvis in three pieces.

'It's nothing Dad. You trump me.'

'Hah.'

Pavarotti's voice rises in exaltation, and Dad lifts my hand, our fingers linked. We both smile and for once, it is uncomplicated between us. That is why I return to this ward. The moment fades with Puccini's final notes. I sit holding the cd sleeve in my hands, and feel his presence in the silence.

Vincero, I will overcome.

The Stone Jar
Chris Lynch

for Tony

       I always thought death, like a cigarette,
was a kind of wasting—the burn & slow
exhaustion of fat, then muscle, then

       sinew, until bone & skin folded cleanly
into dust. Instead I learnt it was filled with fluid, flesh
hysterical & puffy, the cellular machinery working

       overtime, pissing & coughing up
the tar sands of the body.

       Your mind was slower, but just as remorseless,
returning again & again to the great mystery at the bottom of the stone
jar
              of your childhood. I don't know

       why they never told you why, only that you drank
the wine of silence, & the wine, until you mastered the art
                     of going without.

       Life became a kind of penance for things
you'd never done. But you took to it with the fervour
       of the smoker & did whatever was asked,

       whatever was needed. "Everything in time," you'd
say, quietly puffing away like a steward on the back step
waiting for the feast. And having emptied from the vessels

       of your body the sediments of soot & of wine, having
been washed clean in the shower, & watched as we gathered
round your bed to offer love & morphine, having been

>   unsure if it was yours, having loved
> red wine, a kind word, the taste of taro dug
> from hot ashes, & realised what you wanted most
>
>>   was warmth,
>> you drowned in your bed. And in the silent
>> jar of the room: the mystery
>
> begins its work.

Still
Lauren Forner

He had wanted to rush her to hospital but she had waved away his concern. 'I'm not going to be one of those Braxton-Hicks suckers.'

Even so, he urged her to see a midwife friend of his mother's who had been guiding them through the pregnancy. She had phoned him from the hospital: 'They're concerned.'

By the time he had arrived home, the divide between them had already formed. She had carried that knowledge, heavy in her belly, for hours, and he was unprepared for it. She sat at their small breakfast table, her stare vacant. She delivered the news bluntly. 'There's no heartbeat. No movement.'

He opened his mouth, not sure what would tumble out of it, but she did not invite questions.

She presented to him the alternatives the obstetrician had laid out: induction or surgery. He deferred to her judgment, 'It's your body.'

'This thing, is no part of me.' She spat. The stillness inside her had seeped through her flesh, her heart. She, too, was still.

She had chosen surgery. The instruments seemed more clinical, a way to keep the small, unformed being at a distance.

He entered 34A, her narrow room, with its single cupboard and lonely chair. The gerberas swam in the whiteness. His small steps squeaked as he unpacked her belongings.

'Don't bother. I'll be out tomorrow.' The anaesthetic surged through her veins. He could leave her to her drug-induced slumber, now; she would return to him lighter, with the taste of cotton wool in her mouth.

The orderlies wheeled her away and the steel rails glinted at him from the final corner of the corridor. He wandered, after her, then in no direction, around the halls.

Three women stood behind the observation panel next to the nurses' station, wide-eyed. They were three generations of the same genes, their hands rested on the young woman closest to the panel. Her shallow breath fogged the glass and her fingerprints etched themselves into the misted glass. Their collective gaze was focused on the smallest collection of limbs he had ever seen; skin stretched awkwardly over bones that fused at odd angles, a rib cage peaked and dipped without any discernable rhythm. Before he understood his actions, he was there, with them, his own breath clouding the glass.

One of the older women nodded at him, her lips tight and face drawn.

'Which little one's yours?'

He had not noticed the other six newborns in their plastic cots, connected to various monitors. He shook his head in response, the fog catching in his throat. The youngest woman went on staring at her infant but the older two, their eyes layered with grief and struggle, drew him into their fold. They politely looked away as his eyes stung and the saliva in his mouth thickened. They squeezed his hands and the four of them returned to the rise and fall of the small chest in front of them.

Stuff going on while I'm paying rent
Glenn Aljatreux

Well they're stitches but I understand brother,
Because from far away it may as well be barbed wire in my face,
I asked Joseph Smith for protection from my dad,
But he said I'm too busy fucking your friends,
I slept last night with the gulls at the beach to avoid him,

I'm running out Judas,
Some young men feel they are dying at midnight,
Walking in the rain is the only hug from the world,
Her body a church and the heart a bloody temple,
Thank god she is here,

Good morning Department of Human Failure,
I'm going to lie to you about why my soul is spilling over my eyelids,
Foggy and red,
Help is on Jupiter and the knife is in the kitchen drawer,
The real Anton Chigurgh plunged my head into the sink for fun,

Can you please stop spreading jokes about it?
Isn't it enough that my throat is a fleshlight?
Can you please just fucking give me a hug?

Friend?

Cold sweats,
Old Blankets,
Never-dry pillow,
Corner in the room for crouching,
Dry mouth,
Glassy brain,
I need her but shit she's fucking the guy who drives a BMW,

Listen to me brother,
Tell the government lion that our old man used the knife on my nose,
I'm going to be numbing PTSD in the botanical gardens on a bed of beer and cooked grass over the next couple years,

Our youngest sibling is more than her pesticide DNA,
Please you must tell the oldies to not visit the bishop Mr Harris because he asked all of us if we like masturbating,
You must check the crocodiles in your stream,
You must talk,
Or else this will be forever.

Small Things
Cameron Langfield

For Nan

When Pop died, Nan became obsessed with papers.
In her way, she was collecting parts of him

and putting them right. The night
my Pop died, her mourning

came in a single grief-stricken cry.

The next morning, we sat, had breakfast.
She patted the now empty seat

that I could not bring myself to occupy,
and said *How ya doing, Pop.*

It was then I realised her mourning
will come in the washing of his clothes,

or the straightening of his side of the bed, or
the empty seat at the dinner table.

Her mourning will be in the small,
unseen things.

Tears

Marianne Hamilton

I can taste the salt as tears make their way down my cheeks. I lie propped up in this bed, listening to the shrill voice of my mother and the arguments from the kitchen about who is doing the washing up. The voices seem far away, yet they penetrate my consciousness.

My breasts hurt. They hurt so hard because they're full of milk that should be feeding my son. I can't speak. I walk to the doctor to get medicine to stop my milk, but I don't see anything or anyone. I just walk, putting one foot in front of the other. I can still walk.

Eventually we go back to the house and it's weeks before I can bear to go into the nursery and look at the empty cot. But I have other responsibilities. I must look after my other two children who need me. They don't understand, at almost five and three, what has happened.

The night I found him. I can hardly bear thinking of it. Of screaming for the neighbours to come as I tried to resuscitate him, not knowing he was already gone.

The daily chores continue. I fix lunches, mop floors, get dinner, do the laundry. I drive, but in a fog. I can hardly see for my eyes are welling up again, so I pull over. I go out in the car every evening and scream and cry where the boys can't see or hear me. I drive for hours after they sleep, and emerge dry-eyed in the morning to my life.

The smell of jasmine I can't bear as it reminds me of him. It was flowering when I brought him home from hospital. I rip it out when it springs up unbidden in the garden.

Try
Judy Mullen

She snatched the car keys from my hand.

'You could've at least tried,' she snarled at me, storming out.

She had a right to be angry, but I didn't say that.

'Bitch' I muttered.

I don't know if she heard me or not. Would it have made a difference? Not sure, but I tell myself she didn't.

She's right. I could've 'at least tried'. To explain why I came home too late. Again. Tried to stay cool, and just cop it. Let her fling her 'Do you think I wasn't out of mind worrying?' And her 'How much more do you expect me to take?'. And her 'I don't know if I can do this anymore'. That's when I should have tried. To tell her. About the phone call and the hospital and the three hours waiting with him. Until he was safe. She would've understood. She would have leaned in and pulled me to her and held me, and said softly 'Oh Rob, not again.'

Turns out I had 25 minutes. To try. To say 'I know.' And 'I'm sorry.' To try to stop her. From walking out. And getting into the car. To go after her. But I didn't try. Too late.

I'm trying now.

To stop. Seeing the shape of her. At the kitchen bench, stirring her coffee. And tucking her hair behind her ear. To stop looking at the door. Expecting her. To say 'Hi Babe', as if it was all still the same.

I'm trying to stop asking her if she's fed the dog yet. And to stop calling out to her from the lounge room,

'Hey Mel, come and have a look at this . . . .'

I'm trying. To stop. My arm reaching out for her in our bed. To stop smelling her hair on the pillow. To stop aching. To hold her. To stop hearing her voice.

You could've at least tried.

I'm trying hard now. To forget. That she left her coffee cup, half drunk, in the sink. That it's still there, waiting for her. To come back. To take another sip. Just one more sip. I'm trying to forget. That she was up to page 49 of *Big Little Lies*. That she'll never read page 50. To forget that 'bitch' was the last word I said to her.

I am trying now. To remember. That she's gone. To remember to get out of the bed. Everyday. To remember to live. Without her.

I'm trying.

I could have at least tried. To tell her. That she was my only. Reason. To breathe.

Fathom
Nicole Sellers

Balloons scatter over grey storm surf rocking
the playground. We lay flowers, glittery dolphins,
notes. Tremble through speeches. I go home with
my children, aged eight and six, like Cassie and Beau.

From luminous deepfreeze their mother watches us
leave. It was on her birthday he stole them. She grasps
her necklace of classroom jewels and calls it an accident.
Her words churn a rip. Struggling would only drown us all.

At night we go back to the park, swig beer, squint into stinging
spray, pit the swing against the stars, crest the world's underside.

                      I am a dolphin beached at king tide, eyes pecked
                      out. My crow struts. He knows why their father did it.

                    He slams me keyless on the road, arranges bottles, waits.
                    When I wake, a neighbour crouches at the kerb. She shakes
                    her head and ebbs into the dark. Impossible waves roar down
                    the street. You're drunk, say the police, leaving. I drift, like

          coal dust, like bone ash. At school, I hug another mother
              slipping another spat, escaping another town. You
                  hardly knew me, she sneers into the salt
                      wind that weaves our weedy hair.

Sibling gulls rise, cavort in clean sky. I remember
Beau's mane flamed in bus-stop sun, his wry scowl.
Cassie's grit, limping stung through swarming
clover to the soothe of the sea. My daughter

keeps a pink swimsuit Cassie borrowed in her
bottom drawer, and never wears it. My son
keeps a video game Beau played in a living
room, puffs air in its cracks till it breaks. Years

later, I purge the secret struggler's slurry. It's
okay Mum, they say. We thought so, they say.
They go to the beach and dive like dolphins.

Why I can't talk
Eleni Hale

We went to a wedding recently and something unexpected happened. Many of the guests were old, foreign, reminding me of the family I'd left behind in Greece. I stared at the men's faces. That broad dark-eyed look, hands fidgeting with worry beads. And that was when I saw my dad.

He would never grow old. Never smile like that. Never look upon me. He chose something else. Or it chose him.

He left a party suddenly and drove up into the mountains. The same ones he'd go hunting in, one of the few memories I still have of him. He drove up the winding roads, so many opportunities to turn back but he didn't. Through the dark night he went. I know so little.

He may have sat there under that olive tree for hours, the moon shimmering off the metal rifle or he might have done it quick. To guess, I'd say he stayed a while and thought about the years. He was a chronic contemplater like me; someone who drew strange little pictures on the sides of shopping lists and discussed philosophy. These are only fragment memories, I hardly knew him really.

He must have done the calculations and surmised life was no longer worth living. With one shot he extinguished any possibility that might change. Bang! Shattered hope hardens, stiffening the chest. I carry this loss always, forever frozen as is.

Seeing the faces at the wedding I caught a glimpse of what he might have looked like if he'd survived long enough for a deep creasing of the face. A smile and old, wrinkled skin. I was sure he could have been happy if he'd held on.

I can't talk about suicide. Others speak of fathers; the good, the bad and the ugly but I just look away. Sometimes I'm asked where mine is. I say he's dead. Part of me wants them to question how and sometimes they do and I say it straight out, 'He killed himself.' I add, 'It was a long time ago.' But only to make them feel better.

They look shocked and sorry to have asked.

Meanwhile I finally have relief. Air let into a dark, dusty, haunted room. I wish they asked more but they rarely do. I understand. I give a small it's-okay-smile and we move on.

I can't talk about suicide because others can't either. If he was murdered we could discuss crime, offenders and the justice system. We could work our way through blame and solution. Instead it comes back to this. My dad was so sad he died. No one, it seems, could make him happy.

And my personal baggage . . . I didn't rate in this decision.

I can't talk about suicide because time rolls one way. There's nothing that cures. I write this only because I overfill and like drainpipes or blocked sinks, maintenance is required.

If I could talk I'd say, never commit this upon those you love. Never.

Three Unbearable Things
Helen Richardson

I.
A cockatoo sitting on a path in the dirt; the strange posture alerts me
Its eye on me, mine on it. I wait and see some others in a tree
mute and watching. When it finally moves: red spots on white feathers.

Stretches it wings but falls back. I take off my shirt, hold it like a sheet
to capture and rescue but I am too slow, uncertain.
With a cry, a howl, it launches low across the road to a branch nearby.

A white flurry of slashing cries, the watchers alight, catch up, are on it.
It breaks for another higher tree, many more join in the game.
They pull at the bird's wings, extend them like paper fans.

Pecked. Torn. Ragged. Bloody. I scream to drive them off
but can't compete: their screeching is what they do,
my throat unused to it. Grounded, too far below, I brandish my shirt helplessly.

II.

Running, a car door slammed, revving off and barking under the house
Boxing Day the dog emerges, flop eared, wonky, a scratched patch on his rump
Non-returnable. We take him through compassion, our solid companion.

He claims the front seat in the old Landrover, at the park cataracts must
smudge the green, he triangulates by smell, does his business then a strut.
I could never read his brown-black eyes, at the end, shakes his head

blood everywhere, the facial tumour blooming has erupted, he yelps
and cries as they fail to get the catheter in for the killing drugs, the gentler end.
He struggles on, stone-brown eyes imploring. Dumb, stalled, I hover by the door.

III.

I have tried to write this many times, to make my explanations but the ink clogs,
too much, a lifetime, adulterates it. I find her slumped in her chair, can't rouse her.
I stopped to buy flowers, too long. Call the ambulance, speed to emergency before it.

I wait and wait. Regret. Should have ridden with her. Snagged on the wire,
caught, she won't arrive. Will remain always at some point between, while I go on.
Outside the hospital two seagulls, feathers ruffled, stand firm in the wind.

the lactic acid in the calves of your despair
Ali Whitelock

let me pour tea into the holes of your grief, add drops
to your eyes now emptied of tears, wrap your wounds
in gauze soaked overnight in my deepest concern.
let me wring out the sleeves of your thick woollen
jumper now drenched in the song of your mourning.
let me peg it to dry in what little sun there is. let me
utter sounds that comfort, make tea that soothes.
let me know all i can say is
i'm so sorry
here drink this tea
then the sorry thing again.
let me wave you off from the base of the Grampians
of your anguish, fill your back pack with squares of dark
chocolate and emergency dried fruit—nourishment,
you will need it along the way. know as you climb your calves
will burn with the lactic acid of your despair. breathe
into your pain—know it will recede.
sit down a while and drink from the tartan thermos
of your healing. and when you reach your cairn,
lean in to the wind, look down into your valley
of loss. marvel at the distance you have covered.
at how far you have come.

The Hobs of Drought
Jan Iwaszkiewicz

The Loving God's refused to hear a single, crying bleat.
No feed. No water. It is barren on the hobs of drought.
The riverbed is just a craze of mud that's scabbed with sheep.

There is no grace in this. We work along the riverbank
and leave a trail of brass and death. We force ourselves to move.
The eyes beseech, but still we kill and watch the eyes go blank.

The scavengers bear witness to our pain, we use the fence
for them in parodies of crucifixion, twisting each
into the wire with all the anger of our impotence.

We feel it's for the best that we return inside the dark.
Our grief has overlays of shame and so we do not speak.
The dogs are empathetic shadows knowing not to bark.

I sit and clean my rifle with an almost manic care.
A gleaming cartridge rolls between my fingers and it sings,
a song of siren sweetness turning grief into despair.

Grief Is

Kim Anderson

Grief is the colour indigo. Dark, almost black at the centre, like a coagulation of paint fading to a delicate mauve at the edges.

Grief is a black hole of antimatter, heavy beyond comprehension. The emptiness of someone gone outweighs their physical presence because that emptiness is irreversible. The burden of their absence attaches itself to you, invisible yet exhausting.

Grief is confused and surreal. It is cheap shredded tissues and beige walls in a waiting room. Cups of weak tea and hushed voices. Soft-yet-purposeful footsteps along a corridor. Roses in a vase shedding petals, months-old magazines. A final breath, like a sigh. The bottom has dropped out, you are free-falling. What happens now?

Grief settles in the lines around your eyes. It makes your skin taught, like you have leaked everything out and become a dry, empty husk. It squeezes your chest, makes your heart ache and ache. It streaks through your hair and gnaws at your stomach. A face hovers behind your eyelids, already starting to blur. Precious memories linger in your fingertips, the pain of loss felt in the spaces between them.

Grief is a bubble separating you from the afternoon peak traffic and the supermarket queue and the smell of coffee and the children shrieking and the sun shining through the leaves. Inside your soul it is raining.

Grief is a leaden sky, and the last of the leaves falling in an icy gust of wind. It is stillness, and it is a tempest. It is sun beating down upon parched soil, it is a flood engulfing everything in its path. You are lost in a desert, you are adrift on an open sea.

Grief is a photograph on a mantelpiece, it is a bunch of flowers in the rain gathering droplets like tears. It is a fear that if you don't hold them in your thoughts every waking moment, it will be like they never existed.

Grief is a silent scream. Of letting go, and of a refusal to let go. Of regret that you didn't ask all the questions or say all the things until it was too late. Grief rages futilely against our fragility and helplessness, and realises painfully, ultimately, that nothing is permanent.

Grief is hard, grief is soft. It is an agony and a comfort. It is a blanket that suffocates, yet also embraces. It will never leave you, instead eventually settling into the mould of your life like a piece of clay pressed into all the other pieces that make up who you are.

Grief needs to be allowed, not ignored or pushed aside. It will take its course, however long that will be. You will rage against it, you will howl in agony, you will share this feeling with every other person on the planet at some point in time, but in the end you will come through it. And one day you will leave an indigo-coloured hole in someone else's heart, and the cycle will continue.

www.ingramcontent.com/pod-product-compliance
Lightning Source LLC
Chambersburg PA
CBHW070607010526
44118CB00012B/1461